SPORTS PSYCHOLOGY IN PHYSICAL EDUCATION

DR. A. SAKTHIVEL

Dedicated to

my beloved father Mr. A. Arunagiri

and

my mother Mrs. A. Valliammal

Contents

FOREWORD

This book*Sports Psychology in Physical Education* is based on the rivised curriculum of B.P.Ed. The purpose of the book is to provide relevant text to the students. The Book book is written in simple language and easy to understand. The book will provide an authoritative source of information, not only for students, but also for psychologists, researchers and sport coaches.

Authors

ACKNOWLEDGEMENTS

I extend my sincere thanks to Dr. P. Krishnakumar, CEO & Secretary, Nehru Group of institutions, Coimbatore and Dr. B. Anirudhan, Principal, Nehru Arts and Science College(Autonomous), Coimbatore for their immence support.

I express my deepest gratitute to Dr. G. Kumaresan, Associate Professor. Department of Physical Education, Bharathiar University, Coimbatore for his Guidance.

I thank my family members and friends for their support rendered.

I

SPORTS PSYCHOLOGY

Meaning

Sport psychology is a proficiency that uses psychological knowledge and skills to address optimal performance and well-being of athletes, developmental and social aspects of sports participation, and systemic issues associated with sports settings and organizations.

Sport psychology is an interdisciplinary science that draws on knowledge from many related fields including biomechanics, physiology, kinesiology and psychology. It involves the study of how psychological factors affect performance and how participation in sport and exercise affect psychological and physical factors. In addition to instruction and training of psychological skills for performance improvement, applied sport psychology may include work with athletes, coaches, and parents regarding injury, rehabilitation, communication, team building and career transitions.

Scope of sport psychology

Scope of sport psychology instruction and training of psychological skills for performance improvement, applied sport psychology may include work with athletes, coaches, and parents regarding injury, rehabilitation, communication, team building, and career transitions.

- Behaviour
- individual differencess
- heredity and environment
- development stages
- personality and intelligence
- Learning
- measurement and evaluation

Importance of Sports psychology

Sports psychology helps in understanding the behavior of athletes or sportspersons engaged in competitive sports. Coaches also come to know the interest, attitude towards physical activity, instincts, drives and personality of sportspersons. A Sportsperson has some physical limitations in displaying his performance. To overcome these handicaps capacity psychological approach may help the individual to perform beyond his capacity. Physical educationists. coaches and trainers have realized the importance of psychological preparation of athletes, before, during and after the competition. Hence, psychology is emerging as a new branch termed as sports Psychology to achieve better results in sports like:

(1) Analyze the behavior of sportsman and his psychic state.

(2) Identify talent for specific sports.

(3) Create better learning situation.

(4) Knowledge and eligibility of behavior analysis better learning

(5) Stabilizing the performance for a longer period.

(6) Assessing and correcting psychological disorders.

(7) Encouraging the players to make a come back in professional sports

(8) Motivation and learning

(9) Increase of performance& development of tolerance and mental load capacity.

(10) Investigation of sports process& solution of personal and group problem.

(11) Psychological guidance

Stages of Growth and Development:

The growth and development stages of athletes can be grouped into four categories:

- Pre-Adolescence (up to 11 years)
- Early Adolescence (11-13 years)
- Middle Adolescence (14-16 years)
- Late Adolescence (17-19 years)

Type of Individual Differences Psychology

A person differing from others is understandable, but how and why a person differs is less clear and is therefore a subject of the study of individual differences (Revelle, 2000). Individual differences are the differences among individuals, in regards to a single characteristic or number of characteristics, which in their totality distinguish one individual from another and make oneself a unique individual (Mangal, 2007). Characteristics that define individual differences can be classified into four main categories: Learning Style, Aptitude, Personality and Emotional Intelligence.

Learning Style

Learning Style refers to the idea that every individual is different in regards to what manner of coaching or study is most useful for them (Pashler, et al., 2008). Many people tend to realize that they have a unique learning style, and it therefore affects how well they learn under certain circumstances. Some learn best by hearing information, while others see and/or write down information (Cherry, 2012). According to David Kolb; learning involves the gaining of abstract concepts, which are the intangible ideas that can be applied fluidly in a variety of situations (McLeod, 2013). His theory suggests that new experiences provide the necessary drive for the development of new ideas and concepts, which is knowledge.

Kolb's experience-based learning style theory is a four stage learning cycle in which effective learning can only be seen when an individual is able to accomplish all four stages of the cycle (McLeod, 2013). Regardless of where he/she starts first, the individual must go through its logical sequence since each stage is jointly supportive of and moving into the next. The cycle consists of: Concrete Experience Reflective Observation Abstract Conceptualization. Active Experimentation (McLeod, 2013).

Concrete Experience: A new experience or situation is encountered, or a reinterpretation of an existing experience. Reflective Observation: Surveillance of others or developing interpretations about one's own knowledge/experience. Abstract Conceptualization: Daydreaming/Intuition/Reflection leads to a new idea, or a variation of an existing abstract concept - learners create theories to explain observations.

Active Experimentation: The learner applies its knowledge/ experience/observations to the world around them in real time to see its outcome - using theories to explain/answer problems and make proper judgments.

Aptitude

The term aptitude is sometimes treated the same as abilities, particularly when the focus is on prediction of performance in other settings or occasions (Kyllonen & Gitomer, 2002). Abilities are cognitive or mental characteristics that affect one's potential to learn or to perform, whereas aptitude includes any number of individual-differences factors that influence one's willingness or chances of learning or performing successfully (Kyllonen & Gitomer, 2002). Even Aptitude and Intelligence Quotient (IQ) tend to relate in view of human mental ability, however, they are in fact quite the opposite. IQ sees intelligence as being a single measurable characteristic affecting all mental ability, whereas aptitude breaks mental ability down into many different characteristics which are supposed to be more or less independent of each other (wikia.com, 2013).

Similarly - skills, abilities and aptitudes are related but are separate descriptions of what a person can do, and thus, should not be conflated (wikia.com, 2013). Skills are a backward looking description (wikia.com, 2013); it describes what a person has learned to do in the past. Abilities are a present description (wikia.com, 2013); it describes what a person can do now. Aptitudes, however, are a forward looking description (wikia.com, 2013); it describes a person's potential to learn from the past and apply its learning in the future. All these describe what and how a person can learn to do something effectively. It is also assumed that a learner with high aptitude gains knowledge at greater speed with no difficulty, but other learners may not be successful unless they are determined (Alemi, 2006).

Personality

Personality psychologists are interested in the unique characteristics of individuals, as well as relationships among groups of people (Cherry, 2011). A person is able to stand out in the crowd due its personality; this is made up of the characteristic patterns of thoughts, feelings, and behaviors in an individual (Cherry, 2011). While some outer forces can influence how certain characteristics are expressed, personality originates from inside an individual. While a few characteristics of personality may change with age, personality is likely to remain somewhat reliable during the whole life (Cherry, 2011). The major characteristics of personality are:

Personality is Organized and Consistent (Cherry, 2011): People tend to communicate certain features of their personality in various circumstances and their responses are usually stable.

Personality is Psychological, but is influenced by Biological Needs and Processes (Cherry, 2011): While an individual's personality might lead him/her to be calm in normal situations, but when threatened or provoked it might lead him/her to be more aggressive.

Personality 'causes' behaviors to happen (Cherry, 2011): People respond to others and objects in their surroundings based on their personality. From private preferences to choice of profession, every facet of their existence is affected by their personality.

Personality is displayed through thoughts, feelings, behaviors and many other ways (Cherry, 2011): An individual's presence/ existence all together releases energy of good or bad vibes depending on how they connect with all that encompasses their surroundings.

Emotional Intelligence

Emotional Intelligence (EI) is the ability to process emotions (Toyota, 2011); it is the ability to monitor one's own and others' feelings, to differentiate among them, and to use this information to guide one's thinking and action (Salovey & Grewal, 2005). A four-branch model proposed by Mayer and Salovey identifies EI as a set of four related abilities: Perceiving, Using, Understanding, and Managing Emotions (Salovey & Grewal, 2005).

Perceiving Emotions:

The ability to detect and interpret emotions in faces, pictures, voices, and cultural artifacts. It also includes the ability to identify one's own emotions.

Using Emotions:

The ability to control emotions to smooth the progress of various cognitive activities, such as thinking and problem solving.

Understanding Emotions:

The ability to understand emotion language and to value complex affairs among emotions. Furthermore, it includes the ability to recognize and describe how emotions develop over time, such as how shock can turn into grief.

Managing Emotions: Consists of the ability to manage and normalize emotions in both ourselves and in others.

Psychomotor

Psychomotor learning is the relationship between cognitive functions and physical movement. Psychomotor learning is demonstrated by physical skills such as movement, coordination, manipulation, dexterity, grace, strength, speed; actions which demonstrate the fine motor skills such as use of precision instruments or tools.

behavioral examples include driving a car, throwing a ball, and playing a musical instrument . In psychomotor learning research , attention is given to the learning of coordinated activity involving the arms, hands, fingers, and feet, while verbal processes are not emphasized.

II

PERSONALITY

Meaning

Personality is a set of individual differences that are affected by the development of an individual: values, attitudes, personal memories, social relationships, habits, and skills. Different personality theorist present their own definitions of the word based on their theoretical positions. The term "personolity trait" refers to enduring personal characteristics that are revealed in a particular pattern of behaviour in a variety of situations.

Characteristics of Personality

Personality is organized and consistent. We tend to express certain aspects of our personality in different situations and our responses are generally stable. Personality is psychological, but is influenced by biological needs and processes. For example, while your personality might lead you to be shy in social situations, an emergency might lead you to take on a more outspoken and take-charge approach.

Personality *causes* behaviors to happen. You react to the people and objects in your environment based on your personality. From your personal preferences to your choice of a career, every aspect of your life is affected by your personality.

Motivation

Motivation is a theoretical construct used to explain behavior. It gives the reasons for people's actions, desires, and needs. Motivation can also be defined as one's direction to behavior, or what causes a person to want to repeat a behavior and vice versa. A motive is what prompts the person to act in a certain way, or at least develop an inclination for specific behavior.

Types of motivation

Motivation can be divided into two different theories known as *intrinsic* (internal or inherent) motivation and *extrinsic* (external) motivation.

1. **Intrinsic motivation**

Intrinsic motivation has been studied since the early 1970s. Intrinsic motivation is the self-desire to seek out new things and new challenges, to analyze one's capacity, to observe and to gain knowledge. It is driven by an interest or enjoyment in the task itself, and exists within the individual rather than relying on external pressures or a desire for consideration. The phenomenon of intrinsic motivation was first acknowledged within experimental studies of animal behavior. In these studies, it was evident that the organisms would engage in playful and curiosity driven behaviors in the absence of reward. Intrinsic motivation is a natural motivational tendency and is a critical element in cognitive, social, and physical development. Students who are intrinsically motivated are more likely to engage in the task willingly as well as work to improve their skills, which will increase their capabilities. Students are likely to be intrinsically motivated if they:

- attribute their educational results to factors under their own control, also known as autonomy or locus control.
- believe they have the skills to be effective agents in reaching their desired goals, also known as self - efficacy beliefs.
- are interested in mastering a topic, not just in achieving good grades

An example of intrinsic motivation is when an employee becomes an IT professional because he or she wants to learn about how computer users interact with computer networks. The employee has the intrinsic motivation to gain more knowledge. Arts for Art's sake is an example of intrinsic motivation in the domain of artTraditionally, researchers thought of motivations to use computer systems to be primarily driven by extrinsic purposes; however, many modern systems have their use driven primarily by intrinsic motivations. Examples of such systems used primarily to fulfil users' intrinsic motivations, include on-line gaming, virtual worlds, online shopping, learning/education, online dating, digital music repositories, social networking, online pornography, gamified systems, and general gamification. Even traditional management information systems (e.g., ERP, CRM) are being 'gamified' such that both extrinsic and intrinsic motivations must increasingly be considered.

Advantages:

Intrinsic motivation can be long-lasting and self- sustaining. Efforts to build this kind of motivation are also typically efforts at promoting student learning. Such efforts often focus on the subject rather than rewards or punishments.

Disadvantages:

Efforts at fostering intrinsic motivation can be slow to affect behavior and can require special and lengthy preparation. Students are individuals, so a variety of approaches may be needed to motivate different students. It is often helpful to know what interests one's students in order to connect these interests with the subject matter. This requires getting to know one's students. Also, it helps if the instructor is interested in the subject.

1. **Extrinsic motivation**

Extrinsic motivation refers to the performance of an activity in order to attain a desired outcome and it is the opposite of intrinsic motivation. Extrinsic motivation comes from influences outside of the individual. In extrinsic motivation, the harder question to answer is where do people get the motivation to carry out and continue to push with persistence. Usually extrinsic motivation is used to attain outcomes that a person wouldn't get from intrinsic motivation. Common extrinsic motivations are rewards (for example money or grades) for showing the desired behavior, and the threat of punishment following misbehavior. Competition is an extrinsic motivator because it encourages the performer to win and to beat others, not simply to enjoy the intrinsic rewards of the activity. A cheering crowd and the desire to win a trophy are also extrinsic incentives.

Social psychological research has indicated that extrinsic rewards can lead to over justification and a subsequent reduction in intrinsic motivation. In one study demonstrating this effect, children who expected to be (and were) rewarded with a ribbon and a gold star for drawing pictures spent less time playing with the drawing materials in subsequent observations than children who were assigned to an unexpected reward condition. However, another study showed that third graders who were rewarded with a book showed more reading behavior in the future, implying that some rewards do not undermine intrinsic motivation.

While the provision of extrinsic rewards might reduce the desirability of an activity, the use of extrinsic constraints, such as the threat of punishment, against performing an activity has actually been found to increase one's intrinsic interest in that activity. In one study, when children were given mild threats against playing with an attractive toy, it was found that the threat actually served to increase the child's interest in the toy, which was previously undesirable to the child in the absence of threat.

Effects of motivation on sports performance

The first thing is that nobody's perfect! Performing to the best of your ability and challenging yourself each time is tough. The results are often not seen until months or even years of training have taken place. It can be difficult for anyone to stay motivated in the long- term, particularly if they are training solo and have nobody to make them accountable. That's just one example of when motivating coaches and sports motivation speakers can step in.

Motivation is an essential part of sports performance. Self-motivation and extrinsic motivation combined together form the best kind of motivation and encourage goal setting and working hard to reach that goal. So how do you make sure you maximise the benefits of motivation on sports performance for yourself? By understanding exactly how it all works!

How does self-motivation benefit sports performance?

The best thing about self-motivation is you can take it with you anywhere and use it at any time. It's your inner voice and one of the best things to use when training, during a sports match or to gear yourself up before facing a challenge. It's easier said than done at times, particularly if you aren't seeing any visible successes or other areas of your life are interfering in your energy levels. Optimal self-motivation leads to taking that leap, having a go, challenging yourself, and ultimately contributes to a better sports performance where you are sustaining a high-quality engagement while playing.

How does extrinsic motivation benefit sports performance?

Self-motivation is not always enough. What if your inner voice isn't playing ball? What if you need an outer voice to tell your inner voice to wake up? That's where extrinsic motivation is perfect for benefiting your overall sports performance. Good coaching, an encouraging team mate and taking some time out to develop and reinvigorate your sporting goals by attending conferences and hearing sports motivational speakers will all give your extrinsic motivation a boost. This is bound to result in personal sporting success.

Anxiety Meaning

Anxiety is an emotional characterized by an unpleasant state of inner turmoil, often accompanied by nervous behavior, such as pacing back and forth, somatic, complaints and rumination. It is the subjectively unpleasant feelings of dread over anticipated events, such as the feeling of imminent death. Anxiety is not the same as fear, which is a response to a real or perceived immediate threat, whereas anxiety is the expectation of future threat. Anxiety is a feeling of uneasiness and worry, usually generalized and unfocused as an over reaction to a situation that is only subjectively seen as menacing. It is often accompanied by muscular tension, restlessness, fatigue and problems in concentration. Anxiety can be appropriate, but when experienced regularly the individual may suffer from an anxiety disorder.

TYPES OF ANXIETY

1. **Generalised anxiety disorder (GAD)**

A person feels anxious on most days, worrying about lots of different things, for a period of six months or more.

1. **Social phobia**

A person has an intense fear of being criticised, embarrassed or humiliated, even in everyday situations, such as speaking publicly, eating in public, being assertive at work or making small talk.

3. **Specific phobias**

A person feels very fearful about a particular object or situation and may go to great lengths to avoid it, for example, having an injection or travelling on a plane. There are many different types of phobias.

4. **Obsessive compulsive disorder (OCD)**

A person has ongoing unwanted/intrusive thoughts and fears that cause anxiety. Although the person may acknowledge these thoughts as silly, they often try to relieve their anxiety by carrying out certain behaviours or rituals. For example, a fear of germs and contamination can lead to constant washing of hands and clothes.

5. **Post-traumatic stress disorder (PTSD)**

This can happen after a person experiences a traumatic event (e.g. war, assault, accident, disaster). Symptoms can include difficulty relaxing, upsetting dreams or flashbacks of the event, and avoidance of anything related to the event. PTSD is diagnosed when a person has symptoms for at least a month.

6. **Panic disorder**

A person has panic attacks, which are intense, overwhelming and often uncontrollable feelings of anxiety combined with a range of physical symptoms. Someone having a panic attack may experience shortness of breath, chest pain, dizziness and excessive perspiration. Sometimes, people experiencing a panic attack think they are having a heart attack or are about to die. If a person has recurrent panic attacks or persistently fears having one for more than a month, they're said to have panic disorder.

STRESS

Meaning

Stress is often described as a feeling of being overloaded, wound-up tight, tense and worried. We all experience stress at times. It can sometimes help to motivate us to get a task finished, or perform well. But stress can also be harmful if we become over-stressed and it interferes with our ability to get on with our normal life for too long.

Acute stress

Acute stress is the most common form of stress. It comes from demands and pressures of the recent past and anticipated demands and pressures of the near future. Acute stress is thrilling and exciting in small doses, but too much is exhausting. A fast run down a challenging ski slope, for example, is exhilarating early in the day. That same ski run late in the day is taxing and wearing. Skiing beyond your limits can lead to falls and broken bones. By the same token, overdoing on short-term stress can lead to psychological distress, tension headaches, upset stomach and other symptoms.

Fortunately, acute stress symptoms are recognized by most people. It's a laundry list of what has gone awry in their lives: the auto accident that crumpled the car fender, the loss of an important contract, a deadline they're rushing to meet, their child's occasional problems at school and so on. Because it is short term, acute stress doesn't have enough time to do the extensive damage associated with long-term stress. The most common symptoms are:

- Emotional distress — some combination of anger or irritability, anxiety and depression , the three stress emotions.
- Muscular problems including tension headache, back pain, jaw pain and the muscular tensions that lead to pulled muscles and tendon and ligament problems.
- Stomach, gut and bowel problems such as heartburn, acid stomach, flatulence, diarrhea, constipation and irritable bowel syndrome.
- Transient overarousal leads to elevation in blood pressure, rapid heartbeat, sweaty palms, heart palpitations, dizziness, migraine headaches, cold hands or feet, shortness of breath and chest pain.
- Acute stress can crop up in anyone's life, and it is highly treatable and manageable.

Episodic acute stress

There are those, however, who suffer acute stress frequently, whose lives are so disordered that they are studies in chaos and crisis. They're always in a rush, but always late. If something can go wrong, it does. They take on too much, have too many irons in the fire, and can't organize the slew of self-inflicted demands and pressures clamoring for their attention. They seem perpetually in the clutches of acute stress.

It is common for people with acute stress reactions to be over aroused, short-tempered, irritable, anxious and tense. Often, they describe themselves as having "a lot of nervous energy." Always in a hurry, they tend to be abrupt, and sometimes their irritability comes across as hostility. Interpersonal relationships deteriorate rapidly when others respond with real hostility. The workplace becomes a very stressful place for them.

The cardiac prone, "Type A" personality described by cardiologists, Meter Friedman and Ray Rosenman, is similar to an extreme case of episodic acute stress. Type A's have an "excessive competitive drive, aggressiveness, impatience, and a harrying sense of time urgency." In addition there is a "free-floating, but well-rationalized form of hostility, and almost always a deep-seated insecurity." Such personality characteristics would seem to create frequent episodes of acute stress for the Type A individual. Friedman and Rosenman found Type A's to be much more likely to develop coronary heat disease than Type B's, who show an opposite pattern of behavior.

Another form of episodic acute stress comes from ceaseless worry. "Worry warts" see disaster around every corner and pessimistically forecast catastrophe in every situation. The world is a dangerous, unrewarding, punitive place where something awful is always about to happen. These "awfulizers" also tend to be over aroused and tense, but are more anxious and depressed than angry and hostile.

The symptoms of episodic acute stress are the symptoms of extended over arousal: persistent tension headaches, migraines, hypertension, chest pain and heart disease. Treating episodic acute stress requires intervention on a number of levels, generally requiring professional help, which may take many months. Often, lifestyle and personality issues are so ingrained and habitual with these individuals that they see nothing wrong with the way they conduct their lives. They blame their woes on other people and external events. Frequently, they see their lifestyle, their patterns of interacting with others, and their ways of perceiving the world as part and parcel of who and what they are.

Sufferers can be fiercely resistant to change. Only the promise of relief from pain and discomfort of their symptoms can keep them in treatment and on track in their recovery program.

Chronic stress

While acute stress can be thrilling and exciting, chronic stress is not. This is the grinding stress that wears people away day after day, year after year. Chronic stress destroys bodies, minds and lives. It wreaks havoc through long-term attrition. It's the stress of poverty, of dysfunctional families, of being trapped in an unhappy marriage or in a despised job or career. It's the stress that the never-ending "troubles" have brought to the people of Northern Ireland, the tensions of the Middle East have brought to the Arab and Jew, and the endless ethnic rivalries that have been brought to the people of Eastern Europe and the former Soviet Union. Chronic stress comes when a person never sees a way out of a miserable situation. It's the stress of unrelenting demands and pressures for seemingly interminable periods of time. With no hope, the individual gives up searching for solutions.

Some chronic stresses stem from traumatic, early childhood experiences that become internalized and remain forever painful and present. Some experiences profoundly affect personality. A view of the world, or a belief system, is created that causes unending stress for the individual (e.g., the world is a threatening place, people will find out you are a pretender, you must be perfect at all times). When personality or deep-seated convictions and beliefs must be reformulated, recovery requires active self-examination, often with professional help.

The worst aspect of chronic stress is that people get used to it. They forget it's there. People are immediately aware of acute stress because it is new; they ignore chronic stress because it is old, familiar, and sometimes, almost comfortable. Chronic stress kills through suicide, violence, herat attack, stroke and perhaps even cancer. People wear down to a final, fatal breakdown. Because physical and mental resources are depleted through long-term attrition, the symptoms of chronic stress are difficult to treat and may require extended medical as well as behavioral treatment and stress management.

Arousal, Stress & Anxiety

Arousal is general physical and psychological activity. Anxiety is a negative emotional state with feelings of worry, nervousness and apprehension that is associated with the activation of the body. Stress is an imbalance between that demands that someone feels and his or her feelings of capably to meet that demands - when failure of these demands has important consequences.

Arousal can affect performance in many ways. There are several theories as to how stress affects performance. These are summarized in the following:

1. **Drive Theory:**

Drive theory states that the more arousal and anxiety an individual experiences, the higher their performance will be.

2. **Inverted U Hypothesis:**

This theory posits that their is a medium amount of arousal and anxiety that causes one to perform higher - too little anxiety/ arousal and too much anxiety/arousal will cause performance to be poorer.

3. **Individual Zones of Optimal Functioning:**

This theory takes into account that people have different levels of anxiety and arousal that are unique in making them perform at their best. Some people perform their best with low anxiety, some with a medium amount and others with a high amount. The amount of anxiety/arousal that an individual requires to perform their best is based on individual characteristics.

4. **Multidimensional anxiety theory:**

This theory of anxiety posits that when one has anxious thoughts - they will have poorer performance. Anxiety felt by the body will have an effect on performance much like that of the inverted U theory (see above). However, there is little support for this theory.

5. **Catastrophe Model:**

The catastrophe model posits that as long as there are lower thoughts of anxiety, then performance will be best at a medium level of physical arousal. If there is a high level of anxious thoughts (worry), performance will be better at a medium level of physical arousal but will suddenly drop off and become very poor. There is a breaking point when performance decreases dramatically.

6. **Reversal Theory:**

This theory posits that the way that arousal affects performance depends on an individual's interpretation of their arousal. Arousal can be interpreted as pleasant and exciting and as unpleasant and anxious. Arousal that is thought to be pleasant helps performance, and vice versa for bad arousal.

7. **Anxiety direction and intensity:**

This theory states that how someone sees their own anxiety is important for understanding the relationship of their anxiety to their performance. Both the person's interpretation of the intensity (how much anxiety) and the direction (whether the anxiety is helping or hindering their performance) have to be considered. Therefore, viewing anxiety as helpful leads to better performance.

Why Does Arousal Influence Performance?

You may be wondering what it is exactly about arousal that is affecting performance. Arousal increases muscle tension and affects co-ordination. Too much tension can create difficulties. As well, it affects attention. However, attention can become too narrow with too much arousal, and can make one pay attention to too much in their environment when there is too little arousal.

AGGRESSION

Meaning

Aggression is overt, often harmful, social interaction with the intention of inflicting damage or other unpleasantness upon another individual. It may occur either in retaliation or without provocation. In humans, frustration due to blocked goals can cause aggression. Human aggression can be classified into direct and indirect aggression, whilst the first is characterized by physical or verbal behavior intended to cause harm to someone, the second one is characterized by a behavior intended to harm social relations of an individual or a group.

AGGRESSION IN SPORT

In sport, aggression is a characteristic that can have many negative as well as positive effects on performance. Aggression is defined as "any form of behaviour directed toward the goal of harming of injuring another live being who is motivated to avoid such treatment" (Baron & Richardson, 1994). Most people view aggression as a negative psychological characteristic, however some sport psychologists agree that aggression can improve performance (Widmeyer & Birch, 1984). This is called an assertive behaviour (Bredemeier, 1994), where a player will play within the rules of the sport at a very high intensity, but will have no intention to harm an opponent. In sport, aggression has been defined into two categories: hostile aggression and instrumental aggression (Silva, 1983). Hostile aggression is when the main aim is to cause harm or injury to your opponent. Instrumental aggression is when the main aim is achieve a goal by using aggression. For example a rugby player using aggression to tackle his opponent to win the ball. The player is not using his aggression to hurt the opponent but rather to win the ball back. Coulomb and Pfister (1998) conducted a study looking at aggression in high-level sport. They found that experienced athletes used more instrumental aggression in which they used to their advantage and that hostile aggression was less frequently used. Experienced athletes used self-control to help them with their aggression.

A question that can be asked is where does this aggression come from? The frustration aggression theory (Dollard, Doob, Miller, Mowrer, & Sears, 1939) states that aggression occurs because frustration arises due to a goal blockage. However this theory states that every time a player becomes frustrated this will always cause aggression. This theory does not take into account any other intrinsic or extrinsic factors. On the other hand the general aggression model (Anderson & Bushman, 2002) argues that situational and personal factors play a role in causing a person to behave aggressively. Therefore, a player's personality will play a large role in determining whether they are aggressive or not in certain situations. This model also takes into account socially learnt cues and therefore if a player has been taught not to be aggressive in certain situation then he will not use aggression.

It can be seen that aggression comes from a variety of sources and it is important to understand where these sources stem from. Sport stressors allow us to understand what causes an athlete to become frustrated which can lead to aggression and a decline in performance.

In a player's career they will come across a number of high-pressured situations where they will have to deal with many stressors. These can range from personal stressors such as worry and anxiety, to situational stressors such as team-related problems. Much research on stress in sport has been focused on golf and figure skaters, therefore identifying stressors in a team environment is very important (Gould, Jackson & Finch, 1993). Stress can have a negative impact on performance and has been shown to even increase the likelihood of injury (Blackwell & McCullagh, 1990). Noblet and Gifford (2002) studied Australian football players, looking at the different stressors that they experience.

They found that the pressure to perform constantly, poor form and high expectations were all key stressors that affected the players. As well as this, players also found it hard to balance their sport and other commitments. This research can prove very important for psychologists and how they help these players deal with these stressors. In elite sport the main type of stress that has been studied is organisational stress. Shirom (1982) defined organisational stress as "work related social psychological stress".

Woodman and Hardy (2001) investigated organisational stress in elite athletes and they found that there were four main stress issues, which were personal, team, leadership and environmental. Within team issues a large factor that caused stress was tension among athletes. Fletcher and Hanton (2003) conducted a similar study looking at organisational stress and they found that the coach athlete tension was a large contributing factor. Therefore strict coaching and negative feedback can affect performance in many ways. Learning how to deal with stress is key as players must find ways to overcome these problems. In sport psychology, little research has been focused on the coping processes of elite players. It has only just recently been of interest to sport psychologists and is something which needs to be addressed in more detail to improve our understanding (Hardy, Jones & Gould, 1996). Looking at the coping processes of young elite players will allow us to understand how the players deal with stressful situations.

MEASURES OF PSYCHOLOGICAL ASPECTS:

Objective tests, such as self-report measures, rely on an individual's personal responses and are relatively free of rater bias. ... Projective measures are founded in psychoanalytic theories of personality and involve using ambiguous stimuli to reveal inner aspects of an individual's personality.

Learning Objective

- Compare various objective vs. projective personality assessments
- Psychologists seek to measure personality through a number of methods, the most common of which are objective tests and projective measures.

Objective tests, such as self-report measures, rely on an individual's personal responses and are relatively free of rater bias.

- Some of the more idely used personality self- report measures are the Myers-Briggs Type Indicator, Neo Pi-R, MMPI/MMPI-2, 16 PF, and Eysenck Personality Questionnaire.

Projective measures are founded in psychoanalytic theories of personality and involve using ambiguous stimuli reveal inner aspects of an individual's personality.

Apperception

The mind's perception of itself as the subject or actor in its own states, unifying past and present experiences; self-consciousness; perception that reflects upon itself.

Projective Measures

A personality test that is used to identify underlying personality traits; responses are highly subjective.

Validity

The extent to which a concept, conclusion, or measurement is well-founded and corresponds accurately to the real world.

Reliability

The overall consistency of a measure; the likelihood that a measure can be repeated.

MEASURING PERSONALITY:

Psychometrics and Personality Assessment

Test Theory

All scientific theories require measurement of the constructs underlying the field. Personality theories are no different. Whether we are developing theories of species typical behavior, of individual differences in behavior, or unique patterns of thoughts and feelings, we need to be able to measure the responses in question. The fields of psychometrics and personality assessment are devoted to the study of the measurement of pscyhological constructs associated with personality.

Consider the case of differences in vocabulary in a particular language (e.g., English). Although it is logically possible to organize people in terms of the specific words they know in English, the more than 2^(500,000) possible response patterns that could be found by quizzing people on each of the more than 500,000 words in English introduces more complexity rather than less. Classical Test Theory (CTT) ignores individual response patterns and estimates an individual's total vocabulary size by measuring performance on small samples of words. Words are seen as random replicates of each other and thus individual differences in total vocabulary size are estimated from observed differences on these smaller samples. The Pearson Product Moment Correlation Coefficient (r) compares the degree of covariance between these samples with the variance within samples. As the number of words sampled increases, the correlation of the individual differences within each sample and with those in the total domain increases accordingly.

Estimates of ability based upon Item Response Theory (IRT) take into account parameters of the words themselves (i.e., the difficulty and discriminability of each word) and estimate a single ability parameter for each individual. Although CTT and IRT estimates are highly correlated, CTT statistics are based on decomposing the sources of variance within and between individuals while IRT statistics focus on the precision of an individual estimate without requiring differences between individuals. CTT estimates of reliability of ability measures are assessed across similar items (internal consistency), across alternate forms, and across different forms of assessment as well as over time (stability). Tests are reliable to the extent that differences within individuals are small compared to those between individuals when generalizing across items, forms, or occasions. CTT reliability thus requires between subject variability. IRT estimates, on the other hand, are concerned with the precision of measurement for a particular person in terms of a metric defined by item difficulty.

The test theory developed to account for sampling differences within domains can be generalized to account for differences between domains. Just as different samples of words will yield somewhat different estimates of vocabulary, different cognitive tasks (e.g., vocabulary and arithmetic performance) will yield different estimates of performance. Using multivariate procedures such as Principal Components Analysis or Factor Analysis, it is possible to decompose the total variation into between domain covariance, within domain covariance, and within domain variance. One of the most replicable observations in the study of individual differences is that almost all tests thought to assess cognitive ability have a general factor (g) that is shared with other tests of ability. That is, although each test has specific variance associated with content (e.g., linguistic, spatial), form of administration (e.g., auditory, visual), or operations involved (e.g., perceptual speed, memory storage, memory retrieval, abstract reasoning), there is general variance that is common to all tests of cognitive ability.

Statistical programs

Statistical techniques in personality measurement are available in a very powerful (and open source) package, R. Although somewhat intimidating for the casual user, R is a must have for all serious personality researchers. The R project , based upon the S and S+ stats packages, has developed an extremely powerful set of "packages" that operate within one program. Although described as merely "an effective data handling and storage facility [with] a suite of operators for calculations on arrays, in particular, matrices" R is, in fact, a very useful interactive package for data analysis. When compared to most other stats packages used by psychologists, R has at least three compelling advantages: it is free, it runs on multiple platforms (e.g., Windows, Unix, Linux, and Mac OS X and Classic), and combines many of the most useful statistical programs into one quasi integrated program. (R is free software as part of the GNU Project, That is, users are free to use, modify, and distribute the program, within the limits of the GNU non - license). The program itself and detailed installation isntructions for Linux, Unix, Windows, and Macs are available through CRAN.

Aguide to R or the personality researcher as well as a package of functions particularly suited for personality measurement is now part of the personality project. The R suite of programs includes many useful for the personality researcher, including factor analysis, structural equation modeling, and multidimensional scaling. The psych package includes basic tools for scale construction and analysis, including finding basic descriptive statistics, using the Very Simple Structure (VSS) criterion for determing the optimal number of factors , cluster analysis of items using the ICLUST algorithm, hierarchical factor analysis with Schmid Leiman tranformations, and procedures for estimating alternative measures of test reliablility (i.e., alpha, beta, and omega.) All of these functions are available in the psych package which may be downloaded from CRAN. First install R and then install.

III
PRACTICE

The actual application or use of an idea, belief, or method, as opposed to theories relating to it. The customary, habitual, or expected procedure or way of doing of something.

Practice (learning method)

Practice is the act of rehearsing a behavior over and over, or engaging in an activity again and again, for the purpose of improving or mastering it, as in the phrase "practice makes perfect". Sports teams practice to prepare for actual games. Playing a musical instrument well takes a lot of practice. It is a method of learning and of acquiring experience. The word derives from the Greek "πρακτική" (praktike), feminine of " (praktikos), "fit for or concerned with action, practical", and that from the verb "πράσσω" (prasso), "to achieve, bring about, effect, accomplish". In American English, practice is used as both a noun and a verb, but in British English, there is a distinction between practice, used as a noun, and practise, used as a verb (see spelling difference). Sessions scheduled for the purpose of rehearsing and performance improvement are called **practices**. They are engaged in by sports teams, bands, individuals, etc. "He went to football practice every day after school"

Common types of practice

Some common ways practice is applied:

- To learn how to play a musical instrument (musical technique)
- To improve athletic or team performance
- To prepare for a public performance within the performing arts
- To improve reading , writing, interpersonal communication, typing, grammar and spelling.
- To enhance or refine a newly acquired skill
- To maintain skill
- To learn martial arts; Kata and sparring are common forms of practice
- To master tasks associated with one's occupation (e.g. a cashier using a POS system)

How well one improves with practice depends on several factors, such as the frequency it is engaged in, and the type of feedback that is available for improvement. If feedback is not appropriate (either from an instructor or from self-reference to an information source), then the practice tends to be ineffective or even detrimental to learning. If a student does not practise often enough, reinforcement fades, and he or she is likely to forget what was learned. Therefore, practice is often scheduled, to ensure enough of it is performed to reach one's training objectives. How much practice is required depends upon the nature of the activity, and upon each individual. Some people improve on a particular activity faster than others. Practice in an instructional setting may be effective if repeated only 1 time (for some simple verbal information) or 3 times (for concepts), or it may be practised many times before evaluation (a dance movement).

Deliberate practice

People believe that because expert performance is qualitatively different from a normal performance the expert performer must be endowed with characteristics qualitatively different from those of normal adults. We agree that expert performance is qualitatively different from normal performance and even that expert performers have characteristics and abilities that are qualitatively different from or at least outside the range of those of normal adults. However, we deny that these differences are immutable, that is, due to innate talent. Only a few exceptions, most notably height, are genetically prescribed. Instead, we argue that the differences between expert performers and normal adults reflect a life-long period of deliberate effort to improve performance in a specific domain.

One of Ericsson's core findings is that how expert one becomes at a skill has more to do with how one practices than with merely performing a skill a large number of times. An expert breaks down the skills that are required to be expert and focuses on improving those skill chunks during practice or day-to-day activities, often paired with immediate coaching feedback. Another important feature of deliberate practice lies in continually practicing a skill at more challenging levels with the intention of mastering it. Deliberate practice is also discussed in the books Talent is Overrated by Geoff Colvin and The Talent Code by Daniel Coyle,among others.

Two recent articles in *Current Directions in Psychological Science* criticize deliberate practice and argue that, while it is necessary for reaching high levels of performance, it is not sufficient, with other factors such as talent being important as well. In addition, Malcolm Gladwell's point-of-view about deliberate practice is different than Ericsson's view. Gladwell, staff writer at The New Yorker magazine and author of five books on The New York Times Best Seller list including Outliers: The Story of Success said in a May 2016 Freakonomics podcast interview that, "He's [Ericsson] a hard practice guy, and I'm a soft practice guy." Gladwell says that talent is important with an intentional dedication to practice and having a support system is vital to produce superior outcomes. It is not all about methodical effort as Ericsson claims.

Behavioral versus cognitive theories of deliberate practice

Behavioral theory would argue that deliberate practice is facilitated by feedback from an expert that allows for successful approximation of the target performance. Feedback from an expert allows the learner to minimize errors and frustration that results from trial- and-error attempts. Behavioral theory does not require delivery of rewards for accurate performance; the expert feedback in combination with the accurate performance serve as the consequences that establish and maintain the new performance.

In cognitive theory, excellent performance results from practising complex tasks that produce errors. Such errors provide the learner with rich feedback that results in scaffolding for future performance. Cognitive theory explains how a learner can become an expert (or someone who has mastered a domain).

Deliberate practice in medical education

Duvivier et al. reconstructed the concept of deliberate practice into practical principles to describe the process as it relates to clinical skill acquisition. They defined deliberate practice as:

1. Repetitive performance of intended cognitive or psychomotor skills.
2. Rigorous skills assessment
3. Specific information feedback
4. Better skills performance

They further described the personal skills learners need to exhibit at various stages of skill development in order to be successful in developing their clinical skills. This includes:

1. Planning (organize work in a structured way).
2. Concentration/dedication (higher attention span)
3. Repetition/revision (strong tendency to practice)
4. Study style/self reflection (tendency to self- regulate learning)

While the study only included medical students, the authors found that repetitious practice may only help the novice learner (year 1) because as expertise is developed, the learner must focus and plan their learning around specific deficiencies. Curriculum must be designed to develop students‘ ability to plan their learning as they progress in their careers. Finally, the findings in the study also have implications for developing self-regulated behaviors in students. Initially, a medical student may need focused feedback from instructors; however, as Practice as maintenance they progress, they must develop the ability to self-assess.

Practice as maintenance

Skills fade with non-use. The phenomenon is often referred to as being "out of practice". Practice is therefore performed (on a regular basis) to keep skills and abilities honed.

DISTRIBUTED PRACTICE

Distributed practice (also known as spaced repettion or spaced practice) is a learning strategy, where practice is broken up into a number of short sessions - over a longer period of time. Humans and animals learn items in a list more effectively when they are studied in several sessions spread out over a long period of time, rather than studied repeatedly in a short period of time, a phenomenon called the spacing effect. The opposite, massed practice, consists of fewer, longer training sessions. It is generally a less effective method of learning. For example, when studying for an exam dispersing your studying more frequently over a larger period of time will result in more effective learning than intense study the night before.

History

Influential German psychologist Hermann Ebbinghaus first observed the effect of distributed learning, and published his findings in Memory: A Contribution to Experimental Psychology. Using himself as a subject, Ebbinghaus studied lists of nonsense syllables to control for confounding variables such as prior knowledge, allowing him to discover the Spacing effect and serial position effect.

An early study that researched the effects of distributed practice was done by Alan Baddeley and Longman in 1978. They researched the effectiveness of distributed practice by teaching postmen how to type using a new system on a typewriter, and comparing massed and spaced learning schedules. Baddeley found that although massed practice would seem a more effective learning method because the participants would be able to learn the material in fewer days, the postmen who were taught using shorter sessions stretched over multiple days learned the material better than those who had the longer training sessions. Those who learned how to type with shorter learning sessions, spaced over more days ended up with more accurate and quicker typing. Methodology Multiple psychological functions are responsible for the beneficial effects of distributed practice. The most prevalent of these are procedural learning, priming effects and expanding retrieval.

Procedural learning

Procedural learning is the act of repeating a complex activity over and over again, until all of the relevant neural systems work together to automatically produce the activity. Distributed practice is the most efficient method of procedural learning. By equally distributing the amount of practice of a given activity over a period of time, you will increase the efficiency of learning that skill.

Priming

Primingis an effect where an initial (often brief) exposure to a stimulus influences its subsequent recall or perception. This effect is most notable when dealing with semantic knowledge, but is also applicable to the acquisition of general skills. With regards to distributed practice, increasing the amount of practice when learning will result in an increased priming effect for subsequent practice sessions. This causes an increase in memory recall, which is equivalent to an increase in learning. This helps explain why equally distributing your practice sessions, rather than massing them into one session, allows for greater learning.

Expanding Rehearsal

Expanding Rehearsal refers to a learning schedule wherein items are initially tested after a short delay, with pre-test delay gradually increasing across subsequent trials. This phenomenon relies on the strength of the consolidated memory in order to efficiently increase success and learning. Memories that were poorly consolidated through inefficient means of practice will be harder to recall, and will reduce the learning achieved through expanding retrieval. Distributed practice directly influences the efficiency of expanding recall, as it provides the strongest basis for memory consolidation, from which to draw needed information.

Theories of Distributed Practice

Free Recall and Cued-Memory Tasks

Different theories explain the spacing effect in free recall and in explicit cued-memory tasks. Robert Greene proposed a two-factor account of the spacing effect. The spacing effect in free recall tasks is accounted for by the study-phase retrieval account. Because free recall is sensitive to contextual associations, spaced items benefit from additional encoding of contextual information. Thus, the second occurrence of an item in a list reminds the learner of the first occurrence of the same item and of the contextual features surrounding that item. When items are distributed, different contextual information is encoded with each presentation, whereas for massed items, the difference in context is relatively small. This leads to more retrieval cues being encoded with spaced than with massed items, leading to improved recall. Cued-memory tasks (for example, recognitionmemory, and frequency estimation tasks) rely more on item information and less on contextual information. Greene proposed that the spacing effect is due to the increased amount of voluntary rehearsal of spaced items. This is supported by findings that the spacing effect is not found when items are studied through incidental learning.

Semantic Analysis and Priming

Research has also shown reliable spacing effects in cued recall tasks under incidental learning conditions, where semantic analysis is encouraged through orienting tasks.[8][9] Bradford Challis found a spacing effect for target words after the words were incidentally analyzed semantically. However, no spacing effect was found when the target words were shallowly encoded using a graphemic study task. This suggests that semantic priming underlies the spacing effect in cued-memory tasks.

When items are presented in a massed fashion, the first occurrence of the target to be memorized, semantically primes the mental representation of that target, such that when the second occurrence appears directly after the first, there is a reduction in its semantic processing. Semantic priming wears off after a period of time, which is why there is less semantic priming of the second occurrence of a spaced item. Thus, on the semantic priming account, the second presentation is more strongly primed, and receives less semantic processing when the repetitions are massed, compared to when presentations are spaced over short lags. This semantic priming mechanism provides spaced words with more extensive processing than massed words, producing the spacing effect.

Implications with Nonsense Stimuli

From this explanation of the spacing effect, it follows that this effect should not occur with nonsense stimuli that do not have a semantic representation in memory. A number of studies have demonstrated that the semantically-based, repetition priming approach cannot explain spacing effects in recognition memory for stimuli, such as unfamiliar faces, and non-words that are not amenable to semantic analysis. Cornoldi and Longoni have even found a significant spacing effect in a forced- choice recognition memory task when nonsense shapes were used as target stimuli. Russo proposed that with cued memory of unfamiliar stimuli, a short-term perceptually-based repetition priming mechanism supports the spacing effect. When unfamiliar stimuli are used as targets in a cued-memory task, memory relies on the retrieval of structural-perceptual information about the targets.

When the items are presented in a massed fashion, the first occurrence primes its second occurrence, leading to reduced perceptual processing of the second presentation. Short-term repetition-priming effects for nonwords are reduced when the lag between prime and target trials is reduced, thus it follows that more extensive perceptual processing is given to the second occurrence of spaced items relative to that given to massed items. Hence, nonsense items with massed presentation receive less extensive perceptual processing than spaced items; thus, the retrieval of those items is impaired in cued- memory tasks.

Congruent with this view, Russo also demonstrated that changing the font in which repeated presentations of nonwords were presented reduced the short-term perceptual priming of those stimuli, especially for massed items. Upon a recognition memory test, there was no spacing effect found for the nonwords presented in different fonts during study. These results support the hypothesis that short-term perceptual priming is the mechanism that supports the spacing effects in cued- memory tasks when unfamiliar stimuli are used as targets.

Furthermore, when the font was changed between repeated presentations of words in the study phase, there was no reduction of the spacing effect. This resistance to the font manipulation is expected with this two-factor account, as semantic processing of words at study determines performanc e on a later memory test, and the font manipulation is irrelevant to this form of processing.

Mammarella, Russo, & Avons also demonstrated that changing the orientation of faces between repeated presentations served to eliminate the spacing effect. Unfamiliar faces do not have stored representations in memory, thus the spacing effect for these stimuli would be a result of perceptual priming. Changing orientation served to alter the physical appearance of the stimuli, thus reducing the perceptual priming at the second occurrence of the face when presented in a massed fashion. This led to equal memory for faces presented in massed and spaced fashions, hence eliminating the spacing effect.

Encoding Variability

Encoding Variability and assumes the benefits of spacing appear because spaced presentations lead to a wider variety of encoded contextual elements. Additionally, the variable encodings are thought to be a direct result of contextual variations which are not present in massed repetitions.

To test the Encoding Variability theory, Bird, Nicholson and Ringer (1978) presented subjects with word lists that either had massed or spaced repetitions. Subjects were asked to perform various "orienting tasks," tasks which require the subject to make a simple judgement about the list item (i.e. pleasant or unpleasant, active or passive). Subjects either performed the same task for each occurrence of a word or a different task for each occurrence. If the Encoding Variability theory were true, then different orienting tasks ought to provide variable encoding, even for massed repetitions, resulting in a higher rate of recall for massed repetitions than would be expected. The results showed no such effect, providing strong evidence against the importance of Encoding Variability.

Study Phase Retrieval

The study-phase retrieval theory has gained a lot of traction recently. This theory assumes that the first presentation of an item is retrieved at the time of the second presentation. This leads to an elaboration of the first memory trace. Massed presentations do not yield advantages because the first trace is active at the time of the second, so it is not retrieved or elaborated on.

Practical Applications

Spacing Effect and Advertising

The spacing effect and its underlying mechanisms have important applications to the world of advertising. For instance, the spacing effect dictates that it is not an effective advertising strategy to present the same commercial back-to-back (massed repetition).

Appleton-Knapp, Bjork and Wickens (2005) examined the effects of spacing on advertising. They found that spaced repetitions of advertisements are more affected by study-phase retrieval processes than encoding variability. They also found that at long intervals, varying the presentation of a given ad is not effective in producing higher recall rates among subjects (as predicted by variable encoding). Despite this finding, recognition is not affected by variations in an ad at long intervals.

Distributed Practice and Individuals with Memory Deficits

Research shows individuals with traumatic braininjury often suffer memory deficits due to impairment in the acquisition phase. They take far more trials to reach a predetermined learning criterion, but having learned something, their ability to retrieve it is comparable to healthy controls. It is therefore important to aid them in acquiring new skills and memories. Relatively little research has been done examining how learning strategies

which benefit healthy people apply to individuals with TBI.

Gove rover et al. examined the application of the spacing effect in improving functional tasks, such as route learning. Initial performance of the task was better for massed practice, but delayed recall was better for information learned using distributed practice. The longer the delay, the greater the spacing effect. This shows distributed practice has a role in rehabilitation, especially in helping patients with TBI retain new skills. In clinical settings, using word lists, the spacing effect has proven effective with populations of people with memory deficits, including people with amnesia, multiple sclerosis, and TBI.

Long Term Retention with Spacing Effects

Not much attention has been given to the study of the spacing effect in long-term retention tests. Shaughnessy found that the spacing effect is not robust for twice-presented items after a 24-hour delay in testing. The spacing effect is present, however, for items presented four or six times and tested after a 24-hour delay. This seems like a strange result and Shaughnessy interprets it as evidence for a multi-factorial account of the spacing effect.

The long-term effects of spacing have also been assessed in the context of learning a foreign language. Bahrick et. all examined the retention of newly learned foreign vocabulary words over a 9-year period, varying both the number of sessions and the space between them. Both the number of relearning sessions and the number of days in between each session have a major impact on retention (the repetition effect and the spacing effect), yet the two variables do not interact with each other.

For all three difficulty rankings of the foreign words, recall was highest for the 56-day interval as opposed to a 28-day or a 14-day interval. Additionally, 13 sessions spaced 56 days apart yielded comparable retention to 26 sessions with a 14-day interval. These findings have implications for educational practices. Curricula rarely provide opportunities for periodic retrieval of previously acquired knowledge. Without spaced repetitions, students are more likely to forget foreign language vocabulary.

Learning Systems that use Distributed Practice

Distributed learning has been shown to be an effective means to improve learning, and has been applied to many different methods of learning, including the Pimsleur Method and the Leitner System.

Pimsleur Method

The Pimsleur method, or Pimsleur languagelearning system is a language acquisition system developed by Paul Pimsleur which is sold commercially. The Pimsleur Method is based on four principals: Graduated Interval recall, Principal of Anticipation, Core Vocabulary, and Organic Learning. The principal of Graduated Interval Recall is based on the concept of distributed learning, where the learner is presented the information to be learned with gradual increases in the length of time between presentation. It uses the idea that learning can be optimized with a schedule of practice.

The Leitner system is a widely used method of efficiently using flashcards that was proposed by the German science journalist Sebastian Leitner in the 1970s. It exemplifies the principle of spaced repetition, where cards are reviewed at increasing intervals.

In this method, cards are sorted into separate boxes based on how well you know the material on that card. If you succeed in recalling the answer on the card, it is moved into the next box, and if you fail it is moved into a previous box (if there is one). The further into the chain of boxes a card goes, the longer you must wait before attempting to recall its solution. The Leitner method is another example of studying strategies that take advantage of distributed practice and its associated principles, in this case spaced repetition.

Anatomy of Learning

The central biological constructs involved in any kind of learning are those essential to memory formation, particularly those involved with semantic knowledge: the hippocampus and the surrounding Rhinal cortices. Each plays an important role in learning, and therefore in learning techniques such as distributed practice.

Hippocampus

The hippocampus has long been considered the central hub of all memory, and therefore responsible for a large majority of learning. Located in the ventral-medial temporal area of the brain, its importance regarding the consolidation of new memories, and thus the learning of new things, was demonstrated by the infamous case of HM (patient), a man who had both medial temporal regions of his brain removed. This resulted in his inability to form new long-term memories.

The location of the human hippocampus

Despite the overwhelming evidence provided by HM's case for the centrality of the hippocampus to memory and learning, he was still able to benefit from the effects of distributed practice with regards to certain tasks. During H.Ms formal assessment, he displayed notable improvement on tasks regarding unconscious learning such as the mirror-drawing test, where the patient must trace a star by watching their hand in a mirror. His improvement in this and other tasks illustrates that the hippocampus is not essential for all forms of learning, including the ability to benefit distributed practice. Without it, however, improvements are limited. For example, he displayed improvement in the Block-Tapping Memory-Span test, but only to a maximum of 5 blocks, implying his ability to improve through practice continued to exist, but that it does not supersede damage to other aspects of long-term memory formation that he suffered after his surgery.

Distributed learning's effectiveness appears to rely more on one's working memory rather than one's ability to form long term memories. In studies involving the Morris water maze task,rats with hippocampal lesions displaying major reductions in working memory show very little improvement on the test they are working on, despite their supposedly intact ability to form long term memories. This shows that the effects of practice can be essentially removed through reduction in working memory ability

Rhinal Cortex

The Rhinal cortex is an area of the brain surrounding the hippocampus. Multiple animal trials on different species have shown it to be as, if not more important for the existence of multiple different types of memory and learning, than the hippocampus. It is divided into two parts, the Perirhinal cortex and the Entorhinalcortex. Distributed practice exists to a limited degree in animals after the removal of the hippocampus, if the Rhinal cortices are un-damaged.

In summary, damage to either the hippocampus or the rhinal cortices, which result in memory deficits in different areas, also results in a limitation of the effect of distributed practice on learning & memory consolidation, but never completely eliminates it. This shows that the ability to improve learning through distributed practice is not wholly dependent on either the hippocampus or the rhinal cortices but is dependent on the interaction between working memory abilities and the ability to form long- term memories, whether semantic or episodic, conscious or subconscious.

MASSED - DISTRIBUTED PRACTICE

Transcript of Massed vs Distributed Practice

Advantages and Disadvantages of Massed Practice Advantages Features of Massed Practice "This is practising a skill without a break and occurs when an activity is repeated continuously over a period of time with very little or no rest period" (Martin, 2006, p. 167). Examples may include; practising a volleyball serve for 30 minutes practice the various subroutines that make up an overhead serve in volleyball over and over and then practice the whole serve swimming 20 lengths of the pool using a kickboard to concentrate on kicking technique shooting goals for 30 minutes Massed vs Distributed Practice In class we looked at using both Massed and Distributed Practice to develop our skill of serving a volleyball. In these

Perception

Perception (from the Latin perceptio, percipio) is the organization, identification, and interpretation of sensory information in order to represent and understand the environment.[1] All perception involves signals in the nervous system, which in turn result from physical or chemical stimulation of the sense organs. For example, vision involves light striking the retina of the eye, smell is mediated by odor molecules, and hearing involves pressure waves. Perception is not the passive receipt of these signals, but is shaped by learning,memory,expectation, and attention.

Perception can be split into two processes. Firstly, processing sensory input, which transforms these low- level information to higher-level information (e.g., extracts shapes for object recognition). Secondly, processing which is connected with a person's concepts and expectations (knowledge) and selective mechanisms (attention) that influence perception.

Perception depends on complex functions of the nervous system, but subjectively seems mostly effortless because this processing happens outside conscious awareness. Since the rise of experimental psychology in the 19th Century, psychology's understanding of perception has progressed by combining a variety of techniques.

Psychophysics quantitatively describes the relationships between the physical qualities of the sensory input and perception. Sensory neuroscience studies the brain mechanisms underlying perception. Perceptual systems can also be studied computationally, in terms of the information they process. Perceptual issues in philosophy include the extent to which sensory qualities such as sound, smell or color exist in objective reality rather than in the mind of the perceiver.

Although the senses were traditionally viewed as passive receptors, the study of illusions and ambiguousimages has demonstrated that the brain's perceptual systems actively and pre-consciously attempt to make sense of their input. There is still active debate about the extent to which perception is an active process of hypothesis testing, analogous to science, or whether realistic sensory information is rich enough to make this process unnecessary.

The perceptual systems of the brain enable individuals to see the world around them as stable, even though the sensory information is typically incomplete and rapidly varying. Human and animal brains are structured in a modular way, with different areas processing different kinds of sensory information. Some of these modules take the form of sensory maps, mapping some aspect of the world across part of the brain's surface. These different modules are interconnected and influence each other. For instance, taste is strongly influenced by smell.

Definition & Theory.

Perception is the process of recognizing and interpreting sensory stimuli. Learn the definition of perception, how it is related to the five senses, how it differs from reality, and more. Introduction to Psychology: Homework Help Resource / Psychology Courses.

TYPES OF PERCEPTION IN PSYCHOLOGY

The way human beings derive meaning through the senses, including ears, eyes and touch is what makes man to stand out from the rest of the animate beings. Owing to the complexity of deduction depending on what the senses perceive, different kinds of interpretations emerge. It is these that form the different types of perception in psychology that include amodal, color, depth, form, speech, harmonic pitch and rhythmic perceptions.

Amodal Perception

Amodal perception is one of the most recognizable types of perception in psychology. It is the observation and interpretation of things in terms of depth and motion. For instance, even if one sees only three points in a triangular object, he or she knows that the object is three-dimensional and that there are hidden points on the other side.

Color Perception

Color perception, on the other hand, describes the way the visual senses, denoting the eyes, observe hues and contextualize them in the environment. For example, by interpreting blue as the color of depression, the eyes will tend to always attribute all things of this tinge to be melancholic.

Speech Perception

The other types of perception in psychology include those that interpret verbal output. Speech perception, for one, helps in not only understanding one another, but deducing meaning from mere sounds. It also indicates the mechanical arrangement of the vocals when another person speaks which means that the listener interprets the speech through the phonetics such as syllables to create meaning.

Harmonic Perception

Harmonic perception, on the other hand, owes to the understanding that the ear usually perceives inter- related notes, as one, to create meaning in sounds. For instance, riffs in a guitar mixed with those of other instruments lead to interpretation of the music as a single output that is simple to listen to rather than one that actually consists of different notes.

Rhythmic Perception

Rhythmic perception also follows the same theories in its interpretative methodology, whereby the ear gets into a groove by practically responding to it. For instance, one can easily listen to a beat while humming along to it or tapping along as it continues courtesy of its rhythmic harmony.

Depth Perception

Depth perception also acts as one of the types of perception psychology. It relates to the way the human eye identifies and contextualizes things in space. For instance, though the naked eye cannot see the end of a tunnel, it interprets its possible depth through past experiences such as scientific measurements to know how deep the tunnel can be.

Form Perception

Finally, form perception indicates the contextualization of particular objects in a given environment, whereby the eyes sees them as primarily 2- D and at times as 3-D depending on the way of their placement. It is also the understanding of what characterizes the inner and outer core of an object. After seeing an orange, one immediately knows that it is round and has a rough texture on the skin that protects the soft interior.

Therefore, there are different types of perception psychology, each of which with its own interpretative characteristics. The senses can create meaning out of everything by noting characteristics such as depth and form. Understanding music and human speech also uses the senses as a basis of deducting meaning from the respective vocal and musical gestures.

What are the different factors influencing perception?

Perception is our sensory experience of the world around us and involves both the recognition of environmental stimuli and action in response to these stimuli. Through the perceptual process, we gain information about properties and elements of the environment that are critical to our survival. A number of factors operate to shape and sometimes distort perception.

These factors can reside:

- In the perceiver
- In the Object or target being perceived or
- In the context of the situation in which the perception is made.

1. Characteristics of the Perceiver:

Several characteristics of the perceiver can affect perception. When an individual looks at a target and attempts to interpret what he or she stands for, that interpretation is heavily influenced by personal characteristics of the individual perceiver. The major characteristics of the perceiver influencing perception are:

a. Attitudes:

The perciver's attitudes affect perception. For example, Mr. X is interviewing candidates for a very important position in his organization - a position that requires negotiating contracts with suppliers, most of whom are male. Mr. X may feel that women are not capable of holding their own in tough negotiations. This attitude with doubtless affect his perceptions of the female candidates he interviews.

b. Moods:

Moods can have a strong influence on the way we perceive someone. We think differently when we are happy than we do when we are depressed. In addition, we remember information that is consistent with our mood state better than information that is inconsistent with our mood state. When in a positive mood, we form more positive impressions of other. When in a negative mood, we tend to evaluate others unfavourably.

c. **Motives**:

Unsatisfied needs or motives stimulate individuals and may exert a strong influence on their perceptions. For example, in an organizational context, a boss who is insecure perceives a sub ordinate's efforts to do an outstanding job as a threat to his or her own position. Personal insecurity can be translated into the perception that others are out to "get my job", regardless of the intention of the subordinates.

d.Self - Concept:

Another factor that can affect social perception is the perceivers self-concept. An individual with a positive self-concept tends to notice positive attributes in another person. In contrast, a negative self-concept can lead a perceiver to pick out negative traits in another person. Greater understanding of self allows us to have more accurate perceptions of others.

e. **Interest:**

The focus of our attention appears to be influenced by our interests. Because our individual interests differ considerably, what one person notices in a situation can differ from what other perceive. For example, the supervisor who has just been reprimanded by his boss for coming late is more likely to notice his colleagues coming late tomorrow than he did last week.

f. **Cognitive structure:**

Cognitive structure, an individual's pattern of thinking, also affects perception. Some people have a tendency to perceive physical traits, such as height, weight, and appearance, more readily. Cognitive complexity allows a person to perceive multiple characteristics of another person rather than attending to just a few traits.

g. **Expectations:**

Finally, expectations can distort your perceptions in that you will see what you expect to see. The research findings of the study conducted by Sheldon S Zalking and Timothy W Costello on some specific characteristics of the perceiver reveal

- Knowing oneself makes it easier to see others accurately.
- One's own characteristics affect the characteristics one is likely to see in other.
- People who accept themselves are more likely to be able to see favourable aspects of other people.
- Accuracy in perceiving others is not a single skill. These four characteristics greatly influence how a person perceives other int he environmental situation.

2. Characteristics of the Target :

Characteristics in the target that is being observed can affect what is perceived. Physical appearance pals a big role in our perception of others. Extremely attractive or unattractive individuals are more likely to be noticed in a group than ordinary looking individuals. Motions, sound, size and other attributes of a target shape the way we see it. Verbal Communication from targets also affects our perception of them. Nonverbal communication conveys a great deal of information about the target. The perceiver deciphers eye contact, facial expressions, body movements, and posture all in a attempt to form an impression of the target.

3. Characteristics of the Situation:

The situation in which the interaction between the perceiver and the target takes place, has an influence on the perceiver's impression of the target. The strength of the situational cues also affects social perception. Some situations provide strong cues as to appropriate behaviour. In this situation, we assume that + i.e individual's behaviours can be accounted for by the situation, and that it may not reflect the individual's disposition.

FACTORS INFLUENCING PERCEPTION

Perception is a process by which individuals organize and interpret their sensory perceives in order to give meaning to their environment. However, what one perceives can be substantially different from objective reality. There need be, but there is often, disagreement. For example, it's possible that all employees in a firm may view it as great place to work – favorable working conditions, interesting job alignments, good pay, excellent benefits, an understanding and responsible management but, as most of us known, it's very unusual to find such agreement.

Why is perceptiongful picture the world. Perception depends not only on the physical stimuli, but an important in the study of OB? Simply because people's behavior is based on their perception of what reality is, not on reality it self. The world as it is perceived is the world that is behaviorally important. Perception is the process by which an individual selects, organizes, and interprets information inputs to create a meanilso on the stimuli's relation to the surrounding field and on conditions within the individual. The key point is that perception can vary widely among individuals exposed to the same reality. One person might perceive a fast-talking salesperson an aggressive and insincere another, as intelligent and helpful. Each will respond differently to the salesperson.

FACTORS INFLUENCING PERCEPTION:

How do we explain that individuals may look at the same thing, yet perceive it differently? A number of factors operate to shape and sometimes distort perception. These factors can reside in the perceiver in the object or target being perceived, or in the context of the situation in which the perception is made (See Below):

Factors that influence perception: Perception

- Factors in the perceiver
- Attitudes
- Motives
- Interests

- Experience
- Expectations

Factors in the situation

- Time
- Work setting
- Social setting

Factors in the target

  - Novelty
  - Motion
  - Sounds
  - Size
  - Background
  - Proximity
  - Similarity

When an individual looks at a target and attempts to interpret what he or she sees, that interpretation is heavily influenced by the personal characteristics of the individual perceiver. Personal characteristics that affect perception included a person's attitudes, personality motives interest, past experiences, and expectations. For instance if you expect police officers to be authoritative, young people to be lazy, or individuals holding office to be unscrupulous, you may peeve them as such regardless of their cultural traits.

Characteristics of the target being observed affect what is perceived. Loud people are more likely to be noticed in a group than quiet ones. So, too, are extremely attractive or unattractive individuals. Because targets are not looked at in isolation, the relationship of a target to its background also influences perception, as does our tendency to group close things and similar things together. For instance, women people of color or members of any other group that has clearly distinguishable characteristics in terms of features or color are often perceived as alike in other, unrelated characteristics as well.

A shrill voice is never perceived to be one of authority. Practice some vocal exercises to lower the pitch of your voice. Here is one to start: Sing – but do it an octave lower on all your favorite songs. Practice this regularly and after a period of time, your voice will lower. People will perceive you as nervous and unsure if you talk too fast. Also, be careful not to slow down to the point where people feel tempted to finish your sentences.

The context in which we see objects or events is also important. The time at which an object or event is seen can influence attention, as can location, light, heat, or any number of situational factors. For example, at a nightclub on Saturday night, you may not notice a 22 year old female dressed to the nines. Yet that same woman so attired for your Monday morning management class would certainly catch your attention (and that of the rest of the class). Neither the perceiver nor the target changed between Saturday night and Monday morning, but the situation is different.

KINESTHETIC LEARNING OR TACTILE LEARNING

Is a learning style in which learning takes place by the students carrying out physical activities, rather than listening to a lecture or watching demonstrations. People with a preference for kinesthetic learning are also commonly known as "do-ers". The Fleming VAK/ VARKmodel (one of the most common and widely used categorizations of the various types of learning styles) categorized learning styles as follows:

- Hands-on learning
- Visual learning
- Auditory learning
- Read/write learning
- Kinesthetic learning

KINESTHETIC LEARNING IN SPORTS &FITNESS

Kinesthetic Physical Awareness

Wikipedia defines kinesthetic learning as follows; "Kinesthetic learning (also known as tactile learning) is a learning style in which learning takes place by the student carrying out a physical activity, rather than listening to a lecture or watching a demonstration. People with a preference for kinesthetic learning are also commonly known as do-ers." According to Terry Farwell of the Family Education website, "There are three main types of learning: visual, auditory and kinesthetic, which is also known as sensory learning."

Howard Gardner wrote the most intense description of kinesthetic learning in his erstwhile book Frames of Mind: The Theory of Multiple Intelligences. In the 1940's, Margaret H'Doubler was a strong written and oral advocate of kinesthetic learning and the human body's ability to express itself through movement and dance.

We all respond differently to learning. Some of us exceed at more than one of the accepted types of learning. Visual learners learn easily from charts, demonstrations, images and videos. Auditory learners respond well to lectures and discussions. Kinesthetic learners learn best through performing activities like lab tests, role playing and physical activities.

The North Coastal Consortium for Special Education has extensive experience in working with kinesthetic activities. The organisation says that kinesthetic physical awareness, "Refers to the knowledge of your surroundings that you receive via the sensory receptors in your joints, muscles and skin." This corresponds to the information you learn without the use of your eyes. Experts in kinesthetic awareness agree that adults are more skilled at kinesthetic learning than toddlers. Kinesthetic ability does not develop equally in people. We all have different kinesthetic aptitudes.

The Kinetic Chain

The National Sports Academy reports that "All exercises involve the kinetic chain," which is defined as the relationship between one's nerves, muscles and bones. The kinetic chain is divided into two classes:

- **Open Kinetic Chain** – Exercises in this class are performed in non-weight bearing positions. In these exercises, resistance is applied to the end of a limb. This can but does not necessarily cause movement of a joint.

- **Closed Kinetic Chain** – Exercises performed in weight-bearing positions. These exercises are considered more dynamic than open kinetic chain exercises.

For the best results in an exercise routine or in a rehabilitation program, a combination of open and closed kinetic chain exercises is strongly recommended. Even for workouts at a fitness center, the individual should not solely focus on one type of exercise.

Upper Body Exercises

Like most upper body exercises, bicep curls, lateral raises, and triceps extensions and shoulder pendulum exercises are classified as open kinetic chain exercise. These exercises are valuable for sport-specific and weightlifting routines. An individual's shoulder or arm is not considered weight bearing. Upper body closed kinetic chain exercises are extremely helpful in all sorts of rehabilitation programs. These include exercise to improve hand strength and coordination.

There are several popular upper body weight bearing exercises. These include the timeless pushup, forward planks and ball stabilisation exercises. Closed chain exercises are especially favored to protect against injury. They are often used to help heal sprained ligaments.

Lower Body

Closed chain kinetic exercises are popular for sport-specific training and for real-life situations. These weight bearing lower body exercises include squats, lunges, stair-climbing, and single-leg balancing. Lower body open kinetic chain exercises are low impact. Popular exercises in this class include leg curls, leg extensions, hip abduction and hip adduction. These open kinetic chain exercises are popular with those who lift weights and are recommended to increase muscle strength.

Kinesthetics For Improved Balance

Kinesthetics offer many exercises for improving one's balance. They are extremely popular for dancers and athletes. Linda Capuano is an authority on Kinesthetics, recommending it as a good way to test balance. As a starting point, she recommends that you should "stand up tall and close your eyes. If you wobble doing this exercise, which is not uncommon, repeat it until your ability improves." Remember the kinesthetic learning is learning without using your eyes. Once learning to stand on two feet with closed eyes, it is time to improve you balance by closing the eyes and standing on one foot. Alternate feet. The goal should be to sustain your balance for 30 seconds and gradually increase to 60 seconds. Capuano also recommends that that these exercises be practiced in an uncluttered area.

Kinesthetic Exercises for Hands

An excellent way to improve hand and arm movements and mobility is to ask a partner to help. Seat the partner across from you and let them make a number of hand and arm movements. These movements could include pointing a finger, raising an arm or stretching the head. The exercise calls for you to precisely mirror the partner's movements. However, you must keep your eyes focused on the partner's eye's, not on the movements themselves. As you kinesthetic awareness improves, your partner can increase the speed of the motions.

DIFFERENT TYPES OF FEEDBACK

Intrinsic Feedback – Comes from within; proprioceptors and kinaesthesis, concerning the feel of the movement, for example the feeling of the balance during a handstand. This type of feedback is important for autonomous learners who are at a level where they know themselves what needs to be corrected purely by the feeling of the skill. Extrinsic Feedback - Comes from an external source, for example a teacher or coach. This type of feedback is received by seeing and hearing and is used to support intrinsic feedback. Extrinsic feedback is important for beginners/ cognitive learners who have yet to develop the feel of the movement. The feedback can be positive or negative. Positive Feedback – Received when a movement is correctly performed and is used to reinforce the action. Positive feedback can be intrinsic or extrinsic and is used to motivate performers; if they are told by their coach they are performing a skill correctly they will firstly feel an intrinsic reward for being praised and secondly continue to perform the skill to a high level. Positive feedback is even more essential for beginners to motivate them to continue with the learning process.

Negative Feedback – Received when a movement is incorrect in order to prevent the incorrect action being repeated. Negative feedback can be intrinsic of extrinsic. Extrinsic feedback reduces the chance of bad habits developing if given to cognitive and associative learners. Intrinsic negative feedback is used more for more experienced/autonomous performers who may begin to detect and correct their own errors; they need to be making small, specific corrections. The video above is a great example of how to give feedback to young cognitive learners. The coach firstly focuses on the positives of the first half of the game which gains the players' attention towards what the coach is saying because he is praising them, which is ultimately what they want to hear (positive feedback). After explaining to the players what they have done well the coach then adds a way that the performance could have been better or what the players did wrong (negative feedback). Because the players are keen and motivated to do well they will take the negative feedback on board in the hope that their performance will improve further in the next half of the game.

Knowledge of Performance - Concerns the quality of the movement, based on technique; tells you why the movement was correct or incorrect? It can be intrinsic or extrinsic and is important for experienced performers. Knowledge of Results - Concerns the outcome of the movement, based on results; was the movement successful or unsuccessful? It is extrinsic because it comes purely from the success level of the movement, however it can be both positive and negative.

Concurrent Feedback - Received during the movement, both intrinsically and extrinsically.

Terminal Feedback - Received when the movement is complete or after the training session.

Knowledge of results (KR) is defined as extrinsic or augmented information provided to a performer after a response, indicating the success of their actions with regard to an environmental goal. KR may be redundant with intrinsic feedback, especially in real-world scenarios.

Knowledge of resultsis a term in the psychology of learning. A psychology dictionary defines it as feedback of information:

"(a) to a subject about the correctness of [their] responses; (b) a student about success or failure in mastering material, or (c) a client in psychotherapy about progress". It describes the situation where a subject gets information which helps them to change behaviour in a desirable way, or to gain understanding.

There are a number of similar terms in psychology:

- **KCR**: this means "knowledge of correct results". This implies that there is always a specific correct result.
- Operant conditioning and reinforcement: this implies a behaviourist approach using schedules ofreinforcement to "shape behaviour".
- Feedback: this is a more general term, often used for the way systems adjust to preset limits. It is often used in general conversation, with various meanings. Corrective feedback is a version sometimes used in school education.

Knowledge of results, or sometimes immediate knowledge of results, can be used for any learning where a student (or an animal) gets information after the action. The information is about how satisfactory the action is. Memory researchers certainly haven't forgotten **Hermann Ebbinghaus**, the first person to do scientific studies of forgetting, using himself as a subject. He spent a lot of time memorizing endless lists of nonsense syllables and then testing himself to see whether he remembered them. He found that he forgot most of what he learned during the first few hours after learning it.

Later researchers have found that forgetting doesn't always occur that quickly. Meaningful information fades more slowly than nonsense syllables. The rate at which people forget or retain information also depends on what method is used to measure forgetting and retention. **Retention** is the proportion of learned information that is retained or remembered—the flip side of forgetting.

Forgetting Curve

A forgetting curve is a graph that shows how quickly learned information is forgotten over time. Ebbinghaus made use of forgetting curves to chart his research on memory. Measures of Forgetting and Retention Researchers measure forgetting and retention in three different ways: recall, recognition, and relearning.

Recall

Recall is remembering without any external cues. For example, essay questions test recall of knowledge because nothing on a blank sheet of paper will jog the memory.

Recognition

Recognition is identifying learned information using external cues. For example, true or false questions and multiple-choice questions test recognition because the previously learned information is there on the page, along with other options. In general, recognition is easier than recall.

When using the **relearning** method to measure retention, a researcher might ask a subject to memorize a long grocery list. She might measure how long he has to practice before he remembers every item. Suppose it takes him ten minutes. On another day, she gives him the same list again and measures how much time he takes to relearn the list. Suppose he now learns it in five minutes. He has saved five minutes of learning time, or 50 percent of the original time it took him to learn it. His savings score of 50 percent indicates that he retained 50 percent of the information he learned the first time.

Causes of Forgetting

Everyone forgets things. There are six main reasons for forgetting: ineffective encoding, decay, interference, retrieval failure, motivated forgetting, and physical injury or trauma.

Ineffective Encoding

The way information is **encoded** affects the ability to remember it. Processing information at a deeper level makes it harder to forget. If a student thinks about the meaning of the concepts in her textbook rather than just reading them, she'll remember them better when the final exam comes around. If the information is not encoded properly—such as if the student simply skims over the textbook while paying more attention to the TV—it is more likely to be forgotten.

Decay

According to **decay theory**, memory fades with time. Decay explains the loss of memories from sensory and short-term memory. However, loss of long-term memories does not seem to depend on how much time has gone by since the information was learned. People might easily remember their first day in junior high school but completely forget what they learned in class last Tuesday.

Interference

Interference theory has a better account of why people lose long-term memories. According to this theory, people forget information because of interference from other learned information. There are two types of interference: retroactive and proactive.

- **Retroactive interference** happens when newly learned information makes people forget old information.
- **Proactive interference** happens when old information makes people forget newly learned information.

Retrieval Failure

Forgetting may also result from failure to **retrieve** information in memory, such as if the wrong sort of **retrieval cue** is used. For example, Dan may not be able to remember the name of his fifth-grade teacher. However, the teacher's name might suddenly pop into Dan's head if he visits his old grade school and sees his fifth-grade classroom. The classroom would then be acting as a context cue for retrieving the memory of his teacher's name.

Motivated Forgetting

Psychologist Sigmund Freud proposed that people forget because they push unpleasant or intolerable thoughts and feelings deep into their unconscious. He called this phenomenon repression. The idea that people forget things they don't want to remember is also called motivated forgetting or psychogenic amnesia. Anterograde amnesia is the inability to remember events that occur after an injury or traumatic event. Retrograde amnesia is the inability to remember events that occurred before an injury or traumatic event.

COORDINATION ABILITIES IN HUMANS PHYSICAL EDUCATION ESSAY

The word physical refers to the body, and indicates bodily characteristics such as strength, speed, endurance, flexibility, health coordination and performance. It seemingly contrasts the body with mind. The term education when used in conjunction with physical refers to a process of 'education' that develops the human body especially, and the movement skills. Therefore, it transcends all misconceptions and misgivings about physical education as a field of teaching and an ingredient of general education. Human being is an integration of the body and mind. Both components through their combinations make him more successful. The mental process and the physical expression are beautifully interwoven in the mechanism of the whole man and his wholeness in no case should be made to suffer by separating mental and physical aspects (Kamlesh 1988).

Man's life is a continuous flow of activity. Every moment he is doing something and his every activity is the result of the joint efforts of the body and mind; more integrated efforts yield more success to the individual. Things in this world, outside ourselves, come via the body (some organs) into our mind and things in our mind reach the world outside through the body (Sushil Chandra Gupta 1983).

The concept of performance related fitness is an elusive term that has been studied extensively over the past several years, and it has been classified by some experts as an aspect of physical fitness. Balance, coordination, agility, speed of movement, and power are among the most frequently cited components of performance-related fitness (Ali 2005).

COORDINATION MOTOR ABILITIES

Are particularly important at the initial stages of the sports development of a competitor (Zimmermann, Nicklisch,1981, Raczek, 1989, Ljach,1995, Raczek et al., 2002). A high level of coordination improvement since the earliest years makes it possible to make use of technical and tactical skills during a sports competion effectively

(Szczepanik,1993, Ljach,1995, Sadovski, 2003, Starosta, 2003, Gierczuk, 2004). A well-formed basis of Coordination motor abilities in young sportsmen is maintained at a later age and is an important reason for faster and more accurate teaching of other, more difficult movement tasks (Raczek et al., 2002). Especially in sports, in addition to mobility, the coordinative abilities strength, endurance, speed abilities and constitutional conditions are the prerequisites for developing high athletic performance. Starting from a high level of coordinative abilities, athletes can learn and improve athletic motor abilities and techniques that are required for the specific sport more quickly and with a higher degree of quality. (Hartmann et al., 2002).

"Training of proprioception means primarily the training of balance ability. It aims specifically at the improvement of depth perception and the resulting reflex muscle activity and concerns partial aspects of the overall coordinative abilities." (Hafelinger and Schuba 2004). If human beings have to find their balance on an unstable surface, an intra- and intercoordinative reaction of the muscles occurs, which is necessary for maintaining balance. As with proprioception, balancing ability plays a very important role in overall coordination, because the control of movements would be seriously affected without it. This means that balancing ability is also improved and extended through training of proprioception, by being able to learn new movements (Hafelinger and Schuba 2004).

CO-ORDINATION

Means working of all the muscle groups of the body in union. It is of utmost importance in executing any movement with a predetermined objective. Between the muscles groups, co-ordination are divided into inter muscular co-ordination and intra muscular co-ordination. It means coordination between different muscle groups as well as between muscle fibres of the same muscle. Co- ordination is necessary to execute movements requiring speed and strength and more efficiently, therefore, with less expenditure of energy, showing a better performance over a longer time. A person starts losing coordination once he gets tired and vice-versa, a tired person cannot learn movements needing a high degree of co-ordination.

Coordination is the ability to integrate separate motor systems with varying sensory modalities into efficient movements. The harmonious working together of the synchrony, rhythm, and sequencing aspect of one's movements is crucial to coordinated movement. Various parts of the body may be involved, such as eyefoot coordination, as in kicking a ball or walking upstairs. Eye-hand coordination is evident in fine motor activities such as bead stringing, tracing and clay modeling or in gross motor activities such as catching, striking or volleying a ball (Ali 2005).

HAND-EYE COORDINATION

Is the ability of the vision system to coordinate the information received through the eyes to control, guide, and direct the hands in the accomplishment of a given task, such as punching or defending in combat sports. Hand-eye coordination uses the eyes to direct attention and the hands to execute a task. Fine motor skills are involved in the control of small muscle movements, such as when an infant starts to use fingers with a purpose in coordination with the eyes.

Co-ordinative ability should not be equated with motor skills. Though both are inter related and inter dependent upon each other, they are determined by the motor co-ordination process. In a motor skill movement process of body parts are largely automatised for the execution of the particular movement.

The co-ordinative abilities play a vital role to increase the efficiency. To acquire efficiency, we require skilled and efficient potentials, for skilled and efficient potential coordinative abilities are very important and a pre-requisite for performance. It will be useful to children for various sports techniques and for their continuous refinement and modification during the long term training process.

Coordinative abilities are pre-requisites of athletics performance; these are mainly coordinated by motor control process. Athletes' coordinative abilities help them in learning and perfecting technical skill in the training period; the coordinative abilities determine the speed of quality of learning, stabilizing and applying the techniques of sports in coordinative abilities which differ from technical skills that are prerequisite for several motor abilities (Harre, 1989).

The optimal age for motor learning is difficult to define. The conditions seem the best up to early adulthood; however lifelong sensitivity allows motor learning process to continue throughout one's life, in the presence of frequent repetitions and appropriate motivation, depending on the difficulty of the learning task. The periods before puberty are nevertheless to be used particularly intensively for appropriate stimuli (especially with regard to co-ordination and speed), because it makes sense to influence the maturing functions. It has been also proved that co-ordination abilities can be trained particularly well at this age. However this does not mean that no effects can be achieved at more advanced ages. Broad co-ordination seems to be favourable for later success in motor learning (Hirtz & Starosta 2002).

In coordination ability, the control regulation processes are required to function in a particular manner, which is further automatised to a great extent during skill performance. Coordinative abilities have also important and strong links with the motor skills as motor coordination forms the basis of the both. Coordination abilities are understood as relatively stabilized and generalised patterns of motor control and regulation processes. These enable the sportsman to do a group of movements with better quality and effect.

In fact coordinative abilities are understood as stabilized and generalized patterns of motor control and regulation processes. These enable the sportsman to do a group of movements with better utilization and effects. The development of coordinative abilities is important for all sports, but in particular for the technical sports, competitive games and for the combative sports. Seemingly, co-ordinative abilities have no essential significance in sports with standard structures of the movements and relatively constant permanent competitive conditioning. However, purposeful development of coordinative abilities in the given case is one of the determining aspects of sports functioning, on which above all depends the level of the sports technical and tactical mastery. If account is not taken of this, constant specialization in standard form of movement will lead to stagnant motor skills and will narrow the very possibility of their restructuring and renewal (L. Metveyev, 1981).

Seven Coordination motor abilities were assessed on the basis of 14 indices. It was done with the use of sports-motor tests elaborated by various authors (Mynarski, 2000, Raczek et al., 2002). There are seven co-ordinative abilities identified. These are :

(1)Orientation Ability

(2) Differentiation Ability

(3) Coupling Ability

(4) Adaptation Ability

(5) Rhythm Ability

(6) Balance ability and

(7) Reaction Ability.

All the co-ordinative abilities are important for learning of sports techniques and for their continuous refinement and modifications during long term training process. The motor learning ability depends to a large extent on the level of co-ordinative abilities (Hardayal Singh, 1982).

Co-coordinative abilities are primarily dependent on the motor control and regulation process of central nervous system. For each co-coordinative abilities the motor control and regulation process function in a definite pattern when a particular aspect of these functions is improved then the sportsperson is in a better position to do a certain group of movements which for their execution depends on the CNS functioning pattern (Hardayal Singh, 1991).

Eye–hand coordination

Eye–hand coordination (also known as hand– eye coordination) is the coordinated control of eyemovement with hand movement, and the processing ofvisual input to guide reaching and grasping along with the use of proprioception of the hands to guide the eyes. Eye– hand coordination has been studied in activities as diverse as the movement of solid objects such as wooden blocks, archery, sporting performance, music reading, computer gaming, copy-typing, and even tea-making. It is part of the mechanisms of performing everyday tasks; in its absence most people would be unable to carry out even the simplest of actions such as picking up a book from a table or playing a video game. While it is recognized by the term hand–eye coordination, without exception medical sources, and most psychological sources, refer to eye–hand coordination.

IV
LEADERSHIP

Leadership is both a research area and a practical skill encompassing the ability of an individual or organization to "lead" or guide other individuals, teams or entire organizations. The literature debates various viewpoints: contrasting Eastern and Western approaches to leadership, and also (within the West) US vs. European approaches. US academic environments define leadership as "a process of social influence in which a person can enlist the aid and support of others in the accomplishment of a common task". Leadership seen from a European and non-academic perspective encompasses a view of a leader who can be moved not only by communitarian goals but also by the search for personal power.

In a holistic perspective, as the European researcher Daniele Trevisani highlights: "Leadership is a holistic spectrum that can arise from: (1) higher levels of physical power, need to display power and control others, force superiority, ability to generate fear, or group- member's need for a powerful group protector (Primal Leadership), (2) superior mental energies, superior motivational forces, perceivable in communication and behaviors, lack of fear, courage, determination (Psychoenergetic Leadership), (3) higher abilities in managing the overall picture (Macro-Leadership), (4) higher abilities in specialized tasks (Micro-Leadership),

1. higher ability in managing the execution of a task (Project Leadership), and (6) higher level of values, wisdom, and spirituality (Spiritual Leadership), where any Leader derives its Leadership from a unique mix of one or more of the former factors". Studies of leadership have produced theories involving traits, situational interaction, function, behavior, power, vision and values, charisma and intelligence amoung others. power, vision and values, charisma, and intelligence, among others.
2. **DEFINiTION AND MEANING OF LEADERSHIP**

    - The individuals who are the leaders in an organization, regarded collectively.

    - The activity of leading a group of people or an organization or the ability to do this.

Leadership involves:

Establishing a clear vision, sharing that vision with others so that they will follow willingly, providing the information, knowledge and methods to realize that vision, and coordinating and balancing the conflicting interests of all members and stakeholders.

A leader steps up in times of crisis, and is able to think and act creatively in difficult situations.

Different Types of Leadership

According to Research by asaecenter, leadership style is the way a person uses power to lead other people. Research has identified a variety of leadership styles based on the number of followers. The most appropriate leadership style depends on the function of the leader, the followers and the situation. Some leaders cannot work comfortably with a high degree of followers' participation in decision making. Some employers lack the ability or the desire to assume responsibility. Furthermore, the specific situation helps determine the most effective style of interactions. Sometimes leaders must handle problems that require immediate solutions without consulting followers.

What are Different Leadership Styles?

We have covered 12 different types of ways people tend to lead organizations or other people. Not all of these styles would deem fit for all kind of situations, you can read them through to see which one fits right to your company or situation.

1. **Autocratic Leadership**

Autocratic leadership style is centered on the boss. In this leadership the leader holds all authority and responsibility. In this leadership, leaders make decisions on their own without consulting subordinates. They reach decisions, communicate them to subordinates and expect prompt implementation. Autocratic work environment does normally have little or no flexibility. In this kind of leadership, guidelines, procedures and policies are all natural additions of an autocratic leader. Statistically, there are very few situations that can actually support autocratic leadership. Some of the leaders that support this kind of leadership include: Albert J Dunlap (Sunbeam Corporation) and Donald Trump (Trump Organization) among others.

2. **Democratic Leadership**

In this leadership style, subordinates are involved in making decisions. Unlike autocratic, this headship is centered on subordinates' contributions. The democratic leader holds final responsibility, but he or she is known to delegate authority to other people, who determine work projects. The most unique feature of this leadership is that communication is active upward and downward. With respect to statistics, democratic leadership is one of the most preferred leadership, and it entails the following: fairness, competence, creativity, courage, intelligence and honesty.

3. **Strategic Leadership Style**

Strategic leadership is one that involves a leader who is essentially the head of an organization. The strategic leader is not limited to those at the top of the organization. It is geared to a wider audience at all levels who want to create a high performance life, team or organization. The strategic leader fills the gap between the need for new possibility and the need for practicality by providing a prescriptive set of habits. An effective strategic leadership delivers the goods in terms of what an organization naturally expects from its leadership in times of change. 55% of this leadership normally involves strategic thinking.

4. **Transformational Leadership**

Unlike other leadership styles, transformational leadership is all about initiating change in organizations, groups, oneself and others. Transformational leaders motivate others to do more than they originally intended and often even more than they thought possible. They set more challenging expectations and typically achieve higher performance.

Statistically, transformational leadership tends to have more committed and satisfied followers. This is mainly so because transformational leaders empower followers.

5. **Team Leadership**

Team leadership involves the creation of a vivid picture of its future, where it is heading and what it will stand for. The vision inspires and provides a strong sense of purpose and direction. Team leadership is about working with the hearts and minds of all those involved. It also recognizes that teamwork may not always involve trusting cooperative relationships. The most challenging aspect of this leadership is whether or not it will succeed. According toHarvard Business Review, team leadership may fail because of poor leadership qualities.

6. **Cross-Cultural Leadership**

This form of leadership normally exists where there are various cultures in the society. This leadership has also industrialized as a way to recognize front runners who work in the contemporary globalized market.Organizations, particularly international ones require leaders who can effectively adjust their leadership to work in different environs. Most of the leaderships observed in the United States are cross-cultural because of the different cultures that live and work there.

7. **Facilitative Leadership**

Facilitative leadership is too dependent on measurements and outcomes – not a skill, although it takes much skill to master. The effectiveness of a group is directly related to the efficacy of its process. If the group is high functioning, the facilitative leader uses a light hand on the process. On the other hand, if the group is low functioning, the facilitative leader will be more directives in helping the group run its process. An effective facilitative leadership involves monitoring of group dynamics, offering process suggestions and interventions to help the group stay on track.

8. **Laissez-faire Leadership**

Laissez-faire leadership gives authority to employees. According to azcentral, departments or subordinates are allowed to work as they choose with minimal or no interference. According to research, this kind of leadership has been consistently found to be the least satisfying and least effective management style.

9. **Transactional Leadership**

This is a leadership that maintains or continues the status quo. It is also the leadership that involves an exchange process, whereby followers get immediate, tangible rewards for carrying out the leader's orders. Transactional leadership can sound rather basic, with its focus on exchange. Being clear, focusing on expectations, giving feedback are all important leadership skills. According toBoundless.com, transactional leadership behaviors can include: clarifying what is expected of followers' performance; explaining how to meet such expectations; and allocating rewards that are contingent on meeting objectives.

10. **Coaching Leadership**

Coaching leadership involves teaching and supervising followers. A coaching leader is highly operational in setting where results/ performance require improvement. Basically, in this kind of leadership, followers are helped to improve their skills. Coaching leadership does the following: motivates followers, inspires followers and encourages followers.

11. **Charismatic Leadership**

In this leadership, the charismatic leader manifests his or her revolutionary power. Charisma does not mean sheer behavioral change. It actually involves a transformation of followers' values and beliefs.

Therefore, this distinguishes a charismatic leader from a simply populist leader who may affect attitudes towards specific objects, but who is not prepared as the charismatic leader is, to transform the underlying normative orientation that structures specific attitudes.

12. **Visionary Leadership**

This form of leadership involves leaders who recognize that the methods, steps and processes of leadership are all obtained with and through people. Most great and successful leaders have the aspects of vision in them.

However, those who are highly visionary are the ones considered to be exhibiting visionary leadership. Outstanding leaders will always transform their visions into realities.

QUALITIES OF LEADERSHIP

1. **Focus**

"It's been said that leadership is making important but unpopular decisions. That's certainly a partial truth, but I think it underscores the importance of focus. To be a good leader, you cannot major in minor things, and you must be less distracted than your competition. To get the few critical things done, you must develop incredible selective ignorance. Otherwise, the trivial will drown you."

2. **Confidence**

"A leader instills confidence and 'followership' by having a clear vision, showing empathy and being a strong coach. As a female leader, to be recognized I feel I have to show up with swagger and assertiveness, yet always try to maintain my Southern upbringing, which underscores kindness and generosity. The two work well together in gaining respect."

3. **Transparency**

"I've never bought into the concept of 'wearing the mask.' As a leader, the only way I know how to engender trust and buy-in from my team and with my colleagues is to be 100 percent authentically me—open, sometimes flawed, but always passionate about our work. It has allowed me the freedom to be fully present and consistent. They know what they're getting at all times. No surprises."

4. **Integrity**

"Our employees are a direct reflection of the values we embody as leaders. If we're playing from a reactive and obsolete playbook of needing to be right instead of doing what's right, then we limit the full potential of our business and lose quality talent. If you focus on becoming authentic in all your interactions, that will rub off on your business and your culture, and the rest takes care of itself."

5. **Inspiration**

"People always say I'm a self-made man. But there is no such thing. Leaders aren't self-made; they are driven. I arrived in America with no money or any belongings besides my gym bag, but I can't say I came with nothing: Others gave me great inspiration and fantastic advice, and I was fueled by my beliefs and an internal drive and passion. That's why I'm always willing to offer motivation—to friends or strangers on Reddit. I know the power of inspiration, and if someone can stand on my shoulders to achieve greatness, I'm more than willing to help them up."

6. **Passion**

"You must love what you do. In order to be truly successful at something, you must obsess over it and let it consume you. No matter how successful your business might become, you are never satisfied and constantly push to do something bigger, better and greater. You lead by example not because you feel like like it's what you should do, but because it is your way of life."

1. **Innovation**

"In any system with finite resources and infinite expansion of population—like your business, or like all of humanity—innovation is essential for not only success but also survival. The innovators are our leaders. You cannot separate the two. Whether it is by thought, technology or organization, innovation is our only hope to solve our challenges."

1. **Patience**

"Patience is really courage that's meant to test your commitment to your cause. The path to great things is always tough, but the best leaders understand when to abandon the cause and when to stay the course. If your vision is bold enough, there will be hundreds of reasons why it 'can't be done' and plenty of doubters. A lot of things have to come together—external markets, competition, financing, consumer demand and always a little luck—to pull off something big."

3. **Stoicism**

"It's inevitable: We're going to find ourselves in some real shit situations, whether they're costly mistakes, unexpected failures or unscrupulous enemies. Stoicism is, at its core, accepting and anticipating this in advance, so that you don't freak out, react emotionally and aggravate things further. Train our minds, consider the worst-case scenarios and regulate our unhelpful instinctual responses—that's how we make sure shit situations don't turn into fatal resolutions."

4. **Wonkiness**

"Understanding the underlying numbers is the best thing I've done for my business. As we have a subscription-based service, the biggest impact on our bottom line was to decrease our churn rate. Being able to nudge that number from 6 percent to 4 Percent meant a 50 percent increase in the average customer's lifetime value. We would not have known to focus on this metric without being able to accurately analyze our data."

5. **Authenticity**

"It's true that imitation is one of the greatest forms of flattery, but not when it comes to leadership—and every great leader in my life, from Mike Tomlin to Olympic ski coach Scott Rawles, led from a place of authenticity. Learn from others, read autobiographies of your favorite leaders, pick up skills along the way... but never lose your authentic voice, opinions and, ultimately, how you make decisions."

6. **Open-mindedness**

"One of the biggest myths is that good business leaders are great visionaries with dogged determination to stick to their goals no matter what. It's nonsense. The truth is, leaders need to keep an open mind while being flexible, and adjust if necessary. When in the startup phase of a company, planning is highly overrated and goals are not static. Your commitment should be to invest, develop and maintain great relationships."

7. **Decisiveness**

"In high school and college, to pick up extra cash I would often referee recreational basketball games. The mentor who taught me how to officiate gave his refs one important piece of advice that translates well into the professional world: 'Make the call fast, make the call loud and don't look back.' In marginal situations, a decisively made wrong call will often lead to better long-term results and a stronger team than a wishy-washy decision that turns out to be right."

8. Personableness

"We all provide something unique to this world, and we can all smell when someone isn't being real. The more you focus on genuine connections with people, and look for ways to help them—rather than just focus on what they can do for you—the more likable and personable you become. This isn't required to be a great leader, but it is to be a respected leader, which can make all the difference in your business."

9. **Empowerment**

"Many of my leadership philosophies were learned as an athlete. My most successful teams didn't always have the most talent but did have teammates with the right combination of skills, strengths and a common trust in each other. To build an 'overachieving' team, you need to delegate responsibility and authority. Giving away responsibilities isn't always easy. It can actually be harder to do than completing the task yourself, but with the right project selection and support, delegating can pay off in dividends. It is how you truly find people's capabilities and get the most out of them."

10. **Positivity**

"In order to achieve greatness, you must create a culture of optimism. There will be many ups and downs, but the prevalence of positivity will keep the company going. But be warned: This requires fearlessness. You have to truly believe in making the impossible possible."

11. **Generosity**

"My main goal has always been to offer the best of myself. We all grow—as a collective whole—when I'm able to build up others and help them grow as individuals."

12. **Persistence**

"A great leader once told me, 'persistence beats resistance.' And after working at Facebook, Intel and Microsoft and starting my own company, I've learned two major lessons: All great things take time, and you must persist no matter what. That's what it takes to be a leader: willingness to go beyond where others will stop."

13. **Insightfulness**

"It takes insight every day to be able to separate that which is really important from all the incoming fire. It's like wisdom—it can be improved with time, if you're paying attention, but it has to exist in your character. It's inherent. When your insight is right, you look like a genius. And when your insight is wrong, you look like an idiot."

14. **Communication**

"If people aren't aware of your expectations, and they fall short, it's really your fault for not expressing it to them. The people I work with are in constant communication, probably to a fault. But communication is a balancing act. You might have a specific want or need, but it's superimportant to treat work as a collaboration. We always want people to tell us their thoughts and ideas—that's why we have all these very talented people working with us."

15. **Accountability**

"It's a lot easier to assign blame than to hold yourself accountable. But if you want to know how to do it right, learn from financial expert Larry Robbins. He wrote a genuinely humble letter to his investors about his bad judgment that caused their investments to falter. He then opened up a new fund without management and performance fees—unheard of in the hedge fund world. This is character. This is accountability. It's not only taking responsibility; it's taking the next step to make it right."

16. **Restlessness**

"It takes real leadership to find the strengths within each person on your team and then be willing to look outside to plug the gaps. It's best to believe that your team alone does not have all the answers— because if you believe that, it usually means you're not asking all the right questions."

Leadership and the role of a leader in sports

Successful teams have strong leaders and the importance of this role is evident in all categories of sports. The performance of a leader is very clear in interactive games and during matches. Although less obvious in co-active situations, the leader's contribution to the effectiveness of a team's performance is also influential. Leadership maybe considered as a behavioural process that influences individuals and groups towards set goals. As such, a leader has the dual function of ensuring player satisfaction while st he qualities of an effective leader:

There are three traditional types of leadership used in sports varying from an amateur level up to the elite level. Many coaches across team or individual sports will have characteristics from one of these styles if not all.

- Autocratic Leaders
- Democratic Leaders
- Laissez-Faire Leaders

Firstly, the Autocratic style of leadership tends to make all the decisions and is motivated to complete the task as quickly and effectively as possible. This leadership style is 'authoritarian' and does not take into account the opinions or preferences of the group. The autocratic leader will not delegate responsibility and focuses on group performance and achieving groups. This style would be most effective when quick decisions are needed for large groups/ teams i.e. whole team warm up session, when groups are hostile and discipline is needed, in the cognitive stages of learning (Beginners).

Secondly, the Democratic style of leadership tends to share the decisions with the group and is often ready to delegate responsibility. This type of leadership believes in consultation and is interested in developing meaningful interpersonal relationships within the team. The belief is that is that by giving 'ownership' of the task to each individual, the group will work harder, developing unity and a common purpose. This style would be effective in a co-active game or when time constraints are not as exacting , personal support may be required , if groups are small and when in the autonomous stages of learning has been achieved (elite level).

Thirdly, the laissez– faire style, the leader will stand aside and allow the group to make its own independent decisions. This style can happen automatically and will result in a loss of group direction if the leader is inadequate. Lewin (1985) found that when subjected to this style of leadership, group members were inclined to be aggressive towards each other and gave up easily when mistakes occur.

The characteristics adopted by the leader depends fundamentally upon the 'favourableness' of the situation. As is seen in the table below, the most successful teams will have a strong leader, the task is clear and understood by the players and there is a positive relationship between leader and players.

CULTURE MEANING

- The arts and other manifestations of human intellectual achievement regarded collectively. "20th century popular culture" a refined understanding or appreciation of culture. "men of culture"
- The ideas, customs, and social behaviour of a particular people or society.

Physical Culture and Sports

Physical culture is one aspect of the general culture of society; it is a sphere of social activity intended to strengthen personal health, develop one's physical capabilities, and apply the population's physical skills to the service of society. The basic indicators of the level of physical culture in a society are the population's health and physical development and the role of physical culture in upbringing and education, production, everyday life, and the structure of free time; other important indicators are the quality of physical education, the organization of amateur sports, and the winning of major athletic competitions.

The major forms of physical culture are physical exercise; series of physical exercises and exercise competitions; hardening of the body; occupational and everyday hygiene; physical activities such as hiking, cycling, and boating; and physical labor as recreation for people who work at sedentary jobs. In socialist society, physical culture is a right of the people and an important means "of bringing up a new man who harmoniously combines intellectual wealth, moral purity, and physical perfection"

Physical culture promotes the population's involvement in work and public life and raises production efficiency. The physical-culture movement is supported by various state and public organizations, for example, committees of physical education and sports on the all- Union, republic, and oblast levels, trade unions, the Komsomol, voluntary sports societies, the Voluntary Society for Cooperation With the Army, Air Force, and Navy, and sports federations. Such organizations are currently working to open the physical-culture movement to all people, relying on a scientific system of physical education for all social strata.

Numerous countries have state systems of norms and requirements of physical development and fitness for various age groups; for example, the USSR has the program Ready for Labor and Defense of the USSR. Participation in physical-culture activities is a compulsory part of state programs in preschool facilities, all types of educational institutions, and the army.

In various enterprises and institutions, breaks for calisthenics are scheduled as part of the workday. Physical-culture groups have been organized to promote physical culture and hygiene in industrial enterprises, various institutions, kolkhozes, and schools.

In 1976, the USSR had approximately 250,000 such groups, comprising more than 50 million members. These included approximately 120,000 rural groups, with more than 18 million members.

Enrollment in physical-culture and sports groups included more than 20 million in general-education schools, approximately 2 million in vocational and technical schools, more than 2 million in specialized secondary schools, and approximately 2 million in institutes of higher learning. More than 22 million people took part in calisthenics at work, and approximately 7 million belonged to general physical-training groups.

In capitalist society, workers have only limited access to physical culture and to culture in general. In bourgeois states, where the development of physical culture is largely dependent on the interests of monopolies and various business firms, no standard norms for physical education exist, and participation in athletics is impossible for people of most social strata and age groups. An extremely limited number of athletic organizations for working people are sponsored by trade unions.

The numerous stadiums and other sports facilities in capitalist countries belong to bourgeois athletic clubs; membership is prohibitive for the broad masses and in many cases is also traditionally limited by class barriers. As a rule, there is no government subsidy of athletic organizations and sports facilities. The funds set aside for physical culture are primarily for military-applied sports and prestigious spectator sports. Sports, a component of physical culture, are important in physical education. Competitions are held in various series of exercises and training routines. Sports developed historically as a special means of demonstrating and comparing people's physical skills and development.

In the broad sense, the term "sports" comprises athletic training and competition, as well as the specific social relations connected with these activities and the socially significant conditions resulting from them. Sports have considerable social value in that they promote physical fitness, further moral and aesthetic upbringing, and satisfy nonmaterial needs; they are one of the most widespread forms of friendly international relations.

The three basic types of organized sports, which are mutually related, are amateur sports, scholastic sports, and the major sports. Amateur and scholastic sports are important for physical education and the physical fitness of the general population. A person's ability to take part in amateur sports may be somewhat limited by his age, health, and level of physical development. Scholastic sports are taught in all types of educational institutions and are included in army training. Amateur and scholastic sports are important in education and upbringing, practical physical training, health, and recreation. Amateur sports are also the basis for the major sports and are important for the physical development of growing generations.

The major sports provide opportunities for individuals with exceptional talent and skill in a particular sport to set athletic records by undergoing intense specialized and individualized training and by constantly striving to overcome their athletic limitations. They also set standards of excellence for amateur sports and introduce new, effective methods of athletic improvement. Sports records and victories won in official international, national, and other athletic competitions generate a moral stimulus for the development of amateur sports. Each of the numerous sports practiced today has its own particular objective, rules of play, and strategy, usually stressing the players' determination and moral qualities.

Internationally recognized sports are conventionally divided into five basic groups: (1) athletics, or sports based on movement, including track and field, weight lifting, swimming, rowing, ice skating, skiing, boxing, wrestling, fencing, and athletic games; (2) transportation sports, including motorcycle, automobile, airplane, glider, yacht, and ice-boat racing; (3) sports using special equipment for striking a target, such as shooting, trap shooting, and archery; (4) the building and racing of model airplanes, cars, and boats; and

(5) games of intellectual skill for two players, such as chess and checkers.

Sports have historically included various actions derived from everyday life. Sports of ancient origin developed from distinctive physical exercises and movements used in work and battle. Movements used in physical education since ancient times include running, jumping, throwing, weight lifting, rowing, and swimming. Some modern sports evolved in the 19th and 20th centuries from existing sports and related spheres of culture; these include many athletic games, gymnastics, rhythmic gymnastics, the modern entathlon, figure skating, orienteering, and touring. Technical sports came about with the development of technology and include automobile racing, motorcycle racing, cycling, airplane sports, and underwater sports.

Most modern sports that are practiced throughout the world and have commonly accepted procedures and official rules were formalized in the second half of the 19th and first half of the 20th century. At that time official national and international competitions were first held, and national and international athletic associations and sports clubs and societies were formed. In 1896 the largest international sports competition, the Olympic Games, was established, promoting modern sports in most countries of the world. In the mid–19th century professional sports developed, becoming a branch of show business. Professional sports are a business and a source of profit for entrepreneurs and a means of existence for exploited professional athletes.

In socialist countries sports are supported by a mass physical-culture movement. An ever-growing number of people take part in various sports, and the number of sports schools and sports structures and facilities is constantly growing. State and public organizations plan sports programs and set aside considerable sums of money for this purpose. In addition, a well-organized system of athletic competition has been put into effect.

More than 70 sports are practiced in the USSR, including technical and national sports. The most popular sports in the USSR are track and field (as of 1976, more than 6 million persons engaged in sports groups), volleyball (5.2 million), skiing (4.2 million), soccer (3.7 million), basketball (3.5 million), shooting (approximately 3 million), chess (2.8 million), checkers (2.5 million), and table tennis (2.3 million). An average of 0.6–0.7 million persons take part in gymnastics, swimming, handball, and ice hockey. A total of 650,000 persons take part in national sports. The Uniform All-Union Sports Classification determines the successive levels of physical development and technical skill for athletes in various sports from the amateur level to the major sports. Each year as many as 16 million persons fulfill the qualification norms.

High achievement in sports, training, and other athletic activities is encouraged by the conferral of honorary athletic titles, including Master of Sport of the USSR (as of Jan. 1, 1976, held by 108,500 persons), International-class Master of Sport of the USSR (3,500), Honored Master of Sport (more than 2,000), Honored Coach of the USSR (approximately 1,000), and National- class Referee (9,700). Athletes may also receive sports insignia and awards.

The all-Union sports calendar includes as many as 300 different competitions, including national championships in various sports; the Spartakiads of trade unions, the armed forces, and school children; youth and student games; and mass children's competitions, such as the Leather Ball (soccer), the Golden Puck (ice hockey), and the White Rook (chess). In 1956 the first Spartakiad of the Peoples of the USSR was held. These games, held every four years, are the world's largest sports competitions in terms of number of sports and participants; in 1975, 54 million athletes competed, and 7,100 athletes from all the Union republics reached the finals.

In 1976 there were seven all-Union and 30 republic athletic societies, approximately 7,000 sports clubs, approximately 5,000 sports and sports-technical schools for children and young people, and more than 200 specialized higher and secondary schools training teachers of physical education. In addition, there are more than 350 dispensaries for athletes, more than 3,000 stadiums, more than 60,000 gymnasiums, more than 1,300 swimming pools, approximately 500,000 athletic fields, approximately 100,000 soccer fields, more than 18,000 shooting ranges, and approximately 7,000 ski lodges. The volume of sporting goods and equipment produced annually reaches 2 billion items.

One of the most important factors in the development of physical culture and sports is the attention given them in newspapers and magazines, on radio and television, and in films, art, and literature. In 1976 more than 30 sports newspapers and magazines were published. The Fizkul'tura i Sport Publishing House annually puts out more than 250 titles of books and other publications, totaling approximately 17 million copies. Central Television annually devotes as much as 900 hours of broadcasting time to physical culture and sports, and All- Union Radio broadcasts more than 750 hours on the subject.

Since the late 1940's, Soviet athletes have taken part in the international sports movement. In 1976 sports federations of the USSR belonged to 83 international sports associations. From 1948 to 1976, Soviet athletes won 1,936 European championships, 1,391 world championships, and 605 Olympic championships. International sports activities account for more than 30 percent of all cultural ties of the USSR. The USSR maintains sports contacts with more than 90 countries, and the annual exchange of teams and coaches amounts to 40,000 persons. By 1976, the USSR had been host to 44 world championships, 25 European championships, and various other major international competitions.

The decision of the International Olympic Committee to hold the 1980 Summer Olympic Games in Moscow constitutes a worthy evaluation of the level of development of Soviet sports and of the contribution of Soviet athletes to international sports and the Olympic movement. By 1976, more than 2,500 athletes and workers in physical culture and sports had been awarded orders and medals of the USSR for outstanding athletic achievements and service.

Athletes of the USSR and other socialist countries occupy a leading position in world sports, as a result of the social policies of these countries in physical culture and sports. Thus, in the 1976 Summer Olympic Games, athletes from socialist countries were first in 14 sports out of the 24 in the program (the USSR ranking first in eight sports), second in 15 sports, and third in 16 sports. They won 121 of the 198 gold medals, 47 of which were won by the USSR. The ten strongest teams in the Olympic Games included those of the USSR, the German Democratic Republic, the Polish People's Republic, the Socialist Republic of Rumania, the People's Republic of Bulgaria, and the Hungarian People's Republic.

Printed by Libri Plureos GmbH in Hamburg,
Germany